<u>Real Reasons To Impeach Obama</u>

By James Witherspoon

I know this book is going to make a lot of people mad, especially a lot of black people. But before you get the wrong impression I'm not an Obama hater. I love Obama like a brother, a son, or a friend of mine. Regardless, of what I say about Obama, don't think I don't have a lot of love for the brother. Now respect, that's a different thing. The things I don't like about Obama are just that, "things" It isn't personal, it's business.

I'm not a big time author or anything, and I don't have any particular claim to fame. (Not anything I can talk about anyway).I'm just an average black person who never thought much about Politics, one way or the other, because I was always too busy trying to survive and stay alive. I never worried or thought about voting during the civil rights era because it didn't much matter to me who was president of the United States. You know if I didn't care who was president, I damn sure didn't give a flying fuck about Senators, Congressmen, and all the rest of those Political types. I had a reason for this. Mainly I didn't see us "Overcoming "as Martin Luther King kept saying, anytime soon. Not to mention that during that era I was probably too young to vote anyway.

I did however know quite a bit about certain black Politics. By that I mean I was interested in why there always seemed to be something keeping Black people from getting along with each other. When I was growing up, there was what we called in the neighborhood, or the "hood", the "Black Muslims". There was also the NAACP, the Urban League, Martin Luther King JR, Stokely Carmichael, H.rap Brown, and of course, Malcolm X. These are just a few of the Black leaders that I heard about on a regular basis. However, most of these people weren't politicians, they were "Activists", or I guess you could say "Black Activists". I actually had the honor of meeting some of these people in person.

The Black Politicians seemed strange to me because they always somehow managed to keep a safe distance from the likes of Martin Luther, King, the Muslims, (led by The Honorable Elijah Muhammad), who at that time was demanding a separate state for Black people, where naturally he would have been the King. I always thought that was the stupidest thing I had ever heard of, even back then when I was young. I couldn't understand why anyone who Hated, and distrusted, the U.S. government as much as Elijah Muhammad did, would want all of us,(Black Folks), concentrated in one state. I figured the first thing the white folks would do was put us all in one of those dry ass desert States like Arizona, Nevada, or someplace where you couldn't grow anything, and watch our dumb asses starve to death. Then If we complained about anything, declare war on us, and drop a nuclear bomb on our ass.LOL I guess I didn't trust the Government either. My guess was that the Black politicians had to keep a pretty far distance from anybody who was considered "radical "by the Government. Believe it or not, the government considered MLK, a "radical", and to me, he was the most non violent person in the world. His beliefs were what really turned me off about him. I wasn't a bit surprised when they finally admitted that J Edgar Hoover, and the FBI had been wiretapping, and following him all over the country. Maybe I was just being Paranoid, but I thought that any black man with half a brain knew that they were being either wire tapped, or spied on in some other fashion. Remember back in those days the technology was so primitive, you could hear them clicking their equipment on and off, but I thought that was a given fact, I thought everybody knew that. King always gave me the impression that he was "naïve" anyway". King was telling Black people that if a white man hits you, to turn the other cheek. My daddy always told me if anybody hits you, try to kill him, no matter who he was. With King, it was *a religious thing, sort of like Gandhi. I only learned to respect and admire King after I was much older, and finally realized how brave he really was, and how dedicated he was to his people, our people. He really believed in what he was preaching, and to me, that was rare. Plus, King talked that "GOD SHIT", to much for me, and I was an atheist at an early age.*

On the other hand, I had a hard time NOT joining the Black Panthers. They were a REAL "radical" group of young Black men out of Oakland California, who weren't afraid of Shit. They made California change their open carry gun laws when they started doing the same thing that white people were doing, legally carrying their guns out in the open. I think your gun had to be a long gun like a rifle or something, I'm not sure. But, I do know that they changed those laws QUICK, when they saw a lot of Black men walking around openly displaying guns, and there wasn't anything they could do about it. The Idea of Black men

JAMES WITHERSPOON

running around with guns in open public was too much for them to take. We could do the same thing today. All we (Black men), would have to do to change the gun laws is hold a few big rallies all over the country, especially in the red states, and the gun laws would change overnight. It would be really comical to watch the republican lawmakers try to figure out how to pass a law that made it possible for white men to carry guns, but not legal for Black men to carry guns. They would probably try something like they did with the crack cocaine law, where powered cocaine, used mostly by white boys, is nothing more then maybe a fine, and a slap on the wrist, but cheaper crack cocaine, used mostly by black kids in the inner city, is mandatory jail time. Maybe they would go by how much your gun costs. The NRA would love that. I can see them passing a law that says It's OK to carry and display a gun if your gun costs more then say, $1500, and you drive an old pickup truck. That would eliminate most black's right there, because

JAMES WITHERSPOON

very few blacks drive pickup trucks, or trucks of any kind for that matter. But if your gun cost less then $1500 and you drive any "Black Chevy Tahoe "S.U.V" with 20 inch rims on it, you would automatically get 10 yrs in jail. 20 years if you were within a 5 block radius of a school, and 30 years if you was smoking a joint. Obama might even support that if the republicans would say something nice to him.

If you think I was being a little sarcastic about Obama, you're right. You see, I do have a couple of things in common with Obama besides being black, I was born and raised in Chicago, and I also lived in Hyde Park not far from where Obama's house is today. That was after I was older, and married to a Law student. Before that, I lived in all the worst ghettos on the Southside of Chicago. I was also in one of the most notorious Gangs in Chicago. You might say I'm a REAL Chicagoan. There's a big difference between somebody who moves to Chicago from Hawaii, and somebody raised up in *the fucked up streets of Chicago .Boy, I wish I could have been the one from Hawaii. As you can see, I do still have a sense of Humor, sometimes I think that's all I have left. I have to make that distinct difference between us so maybe you can understand the reason I feel the way I do about some of the things I'm going to say about Obama. I also understand that all Black people don't feel the same way that I do about OBAMA, but on the other hand some black people do. I've talked to a lot of black people who told me they were thinking the same thing but felt they were betraying Obama, and other black people. A lot of people don't really know how clannish and racist Black people can be. I'm writing from a Black man's point of view because that's the only view I can give. However, I don't want any white person who might be reading this book, to think I'm just Hating on Obama, or playing "Uncle Tom", because you would be a long way away from the truth. I hate "Uncle Toms" with a passion. I think Clarence Thomas is a* disgrace to humanity, and especially to the Black race. Maybe I'm being a little too hard on Clarence Thomas; I should have said I think the conservative bigots on the SUPREME COURT are a disgrace to humanity. I guess by some of the phrases I'm using you can tell I'm from the "Old "school "as we so fondly call it, but not so old that I don't know the differences between the generations. I know I'm from an older generation, and I have no problem with that. However, I still get a little upset when I hear young white boys, and their young Black friends call each other NIGGER. It's alright for Richard Pryor, Dave Chappell, or Eddie Murphy, to say that as comedians, but for some reason, I can't quite accept it from white people. Maybe I have my own Prejudices, and don't even know it. As a matter of fact, I've always had prejudices against white people because of all the damage they have inflicted on my people, and continue to inflict on us today. However, I'm not dumb enough to think that all white people are the same. The problem is, the ones who make the laws are the same, and think the same way that their ancestors thought. They want to roll back the clock, and take us back to where we started. They think Black people should have no rights, and they have no qualms about saying it. I don't really think that the majority of the white people in the United States think that way, because if they did, Obama would never have been elected president. Not to mention that he was elected TWICE. He was not APPOINTED president like George Bush; He was ELECTED, fair and square. Now let's get started on some of the things I don't like about Obama's ways I agree with a lot of things Obama says and does, however

Here's where I disagree with Obama. Number 1, you don't have to kiss anybody's ass when you have the majority of the people on your side. You have for the most part, some white people, (Democrats) voting for you. You have ALL of the

Black people voting for you, and Most Hispanics, and Asians, (a growing group), voting for you. Yet, you go against your base, and do lots of things not compatible with your base. This is treason against your own base. At one time the Democrats had everything, they had the White House, Congress, and the Senate and Obama squandered it. He was so busy kissing the republicans ass, when all he had to do was push through anything he wanted to do. Instead, all he talked about was bipartisanship. He wanted at least 2 or 3 Republicans to vote on something he really didn't need them for. I remember when Nancy Pelosi announced that "Impeachment for Bush and Cheney is off the table". I knew right then, that Obama and Pelosi were full of shit. Bigger then shit, the next day after, or soon after, Obama announced that he wanted to move forward, not backwards. That was a promise to Bush, and Cheney, that nothing would be done about any of their malfeasance in office. Absolutely nothing was going to be done about the lies that got almost 5,000 American soldiers killed, over 32,000 maimed for life, and over 100,000 Iraqi people murdered by the Bush, and Cheney Administration. I read somewhere the other day that as many as 300,000 people may have died as a direct result of these wars. Nobody is ever going to be held responsible for the war crimes of these devious, murderous, heartless people. I hate to say it, but, Obama is getting exactly what he deserves with Dick Cheney on cable news everyday calling him "weak", ineffective, cowardly, and everything and anything else nasty he can think of. The reason Cheney says this is because he really believes that Obama doesn't have any backbone. He knows that if he had been in Obama's shoes, he would have had Obama facing charges right now for Treason, Murder, lying to the American people to take them into a phony, made up war, you name it. Cheney has every right because he knows that he should have been prosecuted for all the willful, malicious, dirt he has done. Cheney is the kind of person who doesn't respect weakness, and in OBAMAS case, he can't resist the urge to rub shit in Obama's face. Whereas Bush is the kind of person who realizes that he fucked up, and would rather be low key. You can believe that the Secret Service has told Bush, and Cheney both, about how serious it is that neither one of them ever leaves this country again. The press won't talk about the fact that our ex President, and vice president are considered"WAR CRIMINALS" outside of the United States. They won't tell the people that both of them can be arrested, and charged with MASS MURDER, and other war crimes. Cheney wants to change history because he knows History is not going to be nice to him. Yet, he also knows that he has enough of the support of the American Racists in this country who are willing to overlook his faults, and say "let's get rid of that "NIGGER" in our White House." I know I might be using derogatory words that might offend some people, especially Black People, but on the same token, you have to tell it like it is. On one hand, you have Obama, "Afraid of his own shadow" that means he's afraid of the people he is dealing with. Where I come from, you're either a coward, or a MAN. Obama has done a lot of things that I thought he could have done better then he did. He always seemed to want to give the Republicans something to make them "LIKE HIM. What he doesn't seem to understand is that they "HATE HIM". They don't hate him because they don't like his policies, or what party he's in, they "HATE HIM" because he's BLACK, Pure and simple. Obama has given the republicans everything he possibly could, without declaring himself a Republican. He has backed the Wall Street criminals, and bailed out the too big to fail banks, instead of bailing out the people. He has made the income inequality gap jump to record levels. This was brought about because he extended BUSHS tax cuts for the rich. He did that because he thought he would gain some "brownie points" with the republicans if he acted like a republican. If you look at Obama's record, you'll see how he embraces just about everything the republicans stand for. He Kept the Bush tax cuts for the rich; he kept the patriot act, for spying on Americans, and even extended it. He always brags that His healthcare law is a republican Idea. He kept most of "Bush's war mongering generals", (I'll bet they still report to bush and Cheney loyally today as if they still work for them), That's why Cheney has so much to say all the time. He constantly praises Reagan as if he's some kind of 'GOD", which is sickening. I don't think he has any idea how "weak" that makes him look to Democrats, and his base. Lately, he has been bragging about how the well the stock market has been doing since he's been in office, which makes him look foolish, while the poor people get poorer, and the middleclass has all but disappeared. I don't have the time to give you all the different things he has done. It would take me all day. The main thing that bothers me more then anything is the way he sits back casually while hundreds of thousands of young black kids rot in prison, for smoking a joint. These kids have no future. You would think that any black man, in the position he's in, as POTUS, who saw the damage that this was doing, and IS doing, to his people would ACT. The reason I spent so much time explaining myself to mostly Black people is because I want you to understand that I was one of those Black kids without any hope, a long time ago. I spent a lot of unnecessary time in Jail for things I did, and didn't do. I saw a lot of young black men like me in Jail, who were scared to death. I wasn't scared because I was one of those kids the white establishment had branded as a "criminal" at a young age, and had familiarized me with Jail. However, don't get me wrong, Jail is Hell for anybody. When you're in Jail for the first time, you're scared to death. You're worried about people trying to fuck you, and everything else. The first time I went to jail, I was violent, ignorant, and didn't give a fuck. Every time after that I was the same way, until it didn't bother me anymore. At the same time that I was there I saw a lot of other brothers who were not like me. They were scared shitless. They didn't know what to do, they didn't know what to say, they didn't know anything. Now don't get the impression that I was this big, bad, brave motherfucker, in jail. I was just "hooked up". By that I mean I was "well connected ".In other words that you can understand, I knew everybody who was anybody, on the "streets", and were in a powerful position. I knew all of the serious gang leaders, because of my own gang ties. A Lot of the people that the police were locking up, were innocent people, who happened to be in the wrong place at the wrong time. They were simply pawns of a system that cared less then shit about you, especially if you were black. They give you a number because that's all you are to them, a number. You're a number in a system that needs you to support the Jobs of all of the white people in the criminal Justice system. I know there are a few minorities, here and there, that have jobs in the system, but in the big scheme of things they're a minute number. Your jailhouse number supports everything from the piece of shit, Cops on the street, to the prosecutors, to the defense attorneys, the kangaroo court Judges, the guards in the city, state, county, and Federal prisons, etc. You're at the bottom of a system that uses your body as a tool to support another race of people's families. Prisons support entire towns where everybody in town works at the prisons as guards, clerks, librarians, etc, you name it. In Illinois, and other big states around the country, the small towns "BID" for these new prisons to be built in their town because they know everybody in town will get a job there. Thus, in order to have these money making careers, you have to have criminals. If you don't have enough criminals to go around, you have to make them. A sure fire way to accomplish this is through Starvation, Unemployment, depression, discrimination, homelessness, and suppression of other races all across the board. It's no accident that the United States of America has more of its citizens in prison, then any other country in the "WORLD" That includes all of those countries that we've all been brainwashed into hating. Countries like Cuba, Russia, Iran, China, Japan, the entire Middle East, and all of the rest of the world actually. Without those Millions of BROWN, and Black bodies, a lot of white people would be out of JOBS. The Ironic thing about all of this is, that most white people have no idea this is going on. They think Black people are just Criminals, and SHOULD be locked up. That's why I don't blame ALL white people for this travesty of Justice. It's mainly the POLITICIANS who are involved in this conspiracy, and it IS a CONSPIRACY. Obama has never lived this type of life, and doesn't seem to realize how much he is hurting these kids. I know a lot of these kids have got to be wondering why a Black president has no more feelings for them then the white establishment. You don't expect anything from white people, if you do, you will be sadly mistaken. I have a feeling that Obama thinks its safe, to wait until he has nothing to lose, before he will ever free these boys. The reason I say boys, is because most of them are just that "boys." They are NOT hard criminals like I was made to be. They will be a lot worse, and have a lot more HATE then when they first went in. In the meantime, I want to see just how brave Obama is. From What I'm seeing right now, and from what I've seen, it doesn't look good. Obama has no spine. He's so busy kissing the Republicans asses that he doesn't realize that the reason they're giving him such a hard time is partially his own fault. He started out kissing ass, and trying to "go along" to "get along". This is never a good path to follow when you're dealing with ruthless, good for nothing assholes. The more you give in to bullies, the worse they get. I just saw some news on fox cable TV today that said, "Obama's and Eric Holder's justice dept is releasing Hundreds, maybe thousands of drug dealers "into the streets."

They're claiming that Obama through "clemency" is going to infest the streets with Hundreds, or maybe even thousands of black drug dealers. First of all, there are NOT a few hundreds, or thousands of black men and boys in prison for the non crime of smoking a joint. There are "Hundreds of Thousands" of black men in jail for "NOTHING". Plus get this, fox news doesn't want these black dope smoking criminals on the street, they want this injustice to continue. Now before you think Obama is doing something noble and brave for black people, Hold your horses. As we all know, Obama would never do anything to offend republicans or white people in general. Obama has a way of making you think he's doing something when really he's not, for instance; The Qualifications these few men are going to have to meet are this: They have to have ALREADY have spent 10 YEARS for NOTHING, behind bars to even qualify. That's right, 10 years for smoking a joint, or fucking your own head up with some crack. In other words Obama, and his non justice, justice dept are saying it was alright for this racist law, (the mandatory sentencing law) to give them these outrageous sentences in the first place. I guess they're supposed to be thankful. # 2, they have to have had no other criminal history before they were sentenced. If they had no other criminal history before they were sentenced, then why were they even sentenced in the first place? They should have been put on Probation, shouldn't they? #3, they must have a good prison record for the last ten years that they were in prison. Is that a fucking joke? Who in the hell can do 10 yrs behind bars for NOTHING, and not have at least 1 or 2 fights? The first thing you have to do when you go to any jail is establish that you're not a PUNK, because if you don't, you will be a PUNK, when you come out. When I was making my rounds in the jail houses, there was a saying by the inmates, "when you come in here, you'll either come out "SWITCHIN", or BITCHIN".In other words, you're going to be a bad motherfucker, or if you didn't want to fight to protect yourself, they were going to FUCK YOU. Now, will somebody please explain that to Obama, and his "INJUSTICE DEPT"? # 4 you have to have never been associated with anyone in organized crime. Now this one is really crazy. The jails are full of some REAL CRIMINALS, not all of them are innocent kids put there by our hateful, racist, discriminatory laws. Somehow, you're supposed to be a hermit, and pick out all of the Good Guys in jail to hang out with. You're supposed to pick and choose your buddies like you're at summer camp or something. Mr. Obama, and Eric Holder, explain to me how you're going to avoid all of those Gangs, and Gangbangers in Jail? After all, Gangs are organized criminals aren't they, and the prisons are *full of gangs? It just goes to show you how out of touch these people are. They talk like you're off on a 10 year vacation of fun and games, and everybody in jail is just one big happy family. The last I heard, you didn't have much control over your destiny in jail. Much less, hanging out with whoever you wanted to hang out with. That nonsense I saw on cable TV gave me a fucking headache; I'm not going to even finish the rest of the bullshit they said you have to magically do to qualify to get clemency. It's too fucking stupid, and not many people are going to benefit from this bullshit "Clemency" as they call it. What disturbs me is that Obama thinks black people are stupid enough to think he's doing something for them. You have 2 kinds of black people in this country, those who ADMIT that Obama has done nothing for black people, and those that don't ADMIT it. Either way, the republicans make it easy for Obama to bullshit the black people because he always has an excuse NOT to do anything for us.*

JAMES WITHERSPOON

HE has never even made a conscious effort to try to help black people. Mainly, that was because he always knew that we had no choice but to vote for him. The republicans, however strange this might sound, have always been in cahoots with Obama, as far as giving him an excuse not to do anything for his own people. You see, they have kept him on the defense since he has been in office. They have never let up on him, even though they've taken the country down to near total disaster 4 or 5 times. Nothing matters to them except hating Obama, and half of the country agrees with them. Racism is alive and well in this country, and nobody is going to change that anytime soon. The 4th of July was the other day, and I got to thinking. All of this country is celebrating this day, including black people, yet blacks have less to celebrate then anybody. I guess you could say blacks have made a little token progress, but in my eyes, not much. People of all races say "looky there", we have a black president", "now don't that prove that racism is over and done?"

I don't think so. What we have in Obama is a black man afraid of his own shadow. We have a black man who's afraid to show any anger at all, lest he be called an "angry black man". I wonder sometimes does he even have a pulse. He let's people insult him and his family. He let's Bigots like Jan Brewer, the republican governor of Arizona, stick her boney ass skeleton finger in his face. He let's republican congressmen call him a lying ass, black criminal who needs to be impeached. He scrambles to get his birth certificate to prove he was born in this country, knowing that wouldn't satisfy them anyway, no matter what he said or did. It's not like he doesn't know they HATE HIM, it's that he refuses to believe that they really do. He actually thinks he can fight Hate with kindness.

Obama even turns on the very same people who voted for him TWICE. He continues to put as many republicans in high up positions in his cabinet and government positions, as he does DEMOCRATS. I think that has a lot to do with the fact that not many Democrats will defend Obama. The Democrats are wondering why he goes across the aisle so much, and out of his way to find Republicans to fill important positions that he could put democrats in. take for instance; Recently he had to go and find a republican for an important position, so he picked Chuck Hagel. You can't tell me that there's no Democrat that couldn't have filled that position, I don't believe it, and neither do the Democrats. You can't tell me that there were no Democrats that wanted that position I don't believe that. So why did he do that? I will always believe that Obama let so many Democrats down with his spineless reactions to the republicans, that they lost respect for him too, and refused to come out and vote in the 2010 mid term elections. A lot of people, especially Democrats, including me, lost respect when he refused to ram through everything the democrats wanted for that short time they had the house, the senate, and the white house. Obama was so insistent that at least 1 or 2 Republicans vote with the Democrats to show it was a bipartisan vote, that he blew his chances to get a lot of things done. The Democrats were furious that Obama wasted all of that time until Ted Kennedy died, Scott walker was voted in because of lack of effort by a Democratic candidate, and the Republicans had the upper hand .Since then it's been nothing but Obstruction. By the mid terms, Obama didn't have much support from his own people. It also didn't help that Obama and Nancy Pelosi both wanted to play Goody two Shoes and refused to charge Bush, and Cheney with any of the criminal things, and outright lies, that cost the lives of over 100,000 Iraqi people, and the deaths of over 4500 Americans. Not to mention the maimed, on both sides. Bush, and Cheney should both be in prison today, along with Condoleezza Rice, Colin Powell, Rumsfeld, wolfowitz, and all the rest of their murderous gang, for outright lying to the American people, and manufacturing phony evidence to go to war to enrich themselves. However, I have never thought of Obama as a flaming liberal anyway. Actually after listening to him speak for a few months after the election, I didn't think he was even a Democrat. Obama infuriates the hell out of me every time he goes to quoting something that Ronald Reagan said, and how much he admires Reagan. It's sickening, and condescending. I've even heard Republicans express displeasure at him sucking up to Reagan all the time. He does everything he can to kiss the republicans asses, and they don't even appreciate it. It's as if they're trying to tell him, "We HATE you BOY, and there's nothing you can say or do to change that. One of these days I hope to see Obama stand up like a man, and tell them to all "KISS

MY BLACK ASS."However, I guess that's just wishful thinking, I don't think he has it in him. At this point, Obama has nothing to lose, and I notice he's trying to get a little tough on the Republicans. However, this is probably too little, too late, to try to stand up to these bullies. After watching Obama refuse, and afraid to even say "Republican", these last 5 years, I don't guess I should be surprised.

The republicans have Obama scared to even use the word "POOR". The reason This poor man,(no pun intended),is so afraid to even hint at helping POOR PEOPLE, is because he's afraid that if he mentions "poor people", the republicans will say,"AHA", trying to help THOSE Black people huh? We're not going to have none of that are we? What Obama and the Republicans don't seem to either realize, or understand is that most of your POOR PEOPLE are "WHITE", Not Black, not Hispanic, not Asian, but WHITE. Most of the POOR PEOPLE on food stamps are WHITE, NOT BLACK, Asian, Or Hispanic ,Most of the people on any welfare, or social programs are WHITE, including Social Security, Medicare, Medicaid, unemployment insurance, SSI, Disability, etc,. White's outnumber all other races in everything on the receiving end of any welfare distributed to anyone in the United States of America. Yet, that outrageous lie that the republicans spew to their ignorant, Hateful, vote against themselves, white, trailer trash base, is that Blacks and Hispanics are laying around living in the lap of luxury, on food stamps and sucking up all of these IDIOTS hard earned tax money. They actually believe that Minorities have been living like Kings and Queens off the taxes they pay on their $5.15 minimum wage jobs. You know if you can convince these POOR, ASS IDIOTS, that they're taking care of those Lazy, ass, Niggers, and wetbacks, it's real easy to turn the middle class white folks who really DO make a decent living, against the less fortunate amongst us. They've always used divide and conquer tactics against the

American people, this is nothing new. However, you'll never hear this from an elected Republican, or Democrat. The Republicans use this tactic as part of their framework, or makeup. The Democrats just seem to be too weak, and feckless to even expose what they know is true. That's one reason the Dems have no business looking at Obama as weak, because they are just as weak as he is. You'll never hear one of them call out the republicans for the HATE MONGERING, RACISM, Bigotry, and other Vile rhetoric that they're known for. You will find a few Democrats who will go the extra mile to explain the truth to you like Allan Grayson, Howard Dean, Anthony Weiner, and a few others but the Democrats turn on them like Snakes, and automatically go on TV to beg the Republicans not to associate them with these truth telling Democrats. They throw each other under the bus at the drop of a hat.

As much as I enjoy watching MSNBC, the only semi liberal cable channel there is on TV, I've watched in dismay as even ED Shultz, one of my favorites, turn on other democrats. However, I understand that MSNBC is owned by GE a big powerful company that seems to be afraid of libel suits, so they muffle their journalists like outspoken Keith Oberman, Martin Bashir, and a few others, that they fired for being TOO TRUTHFUL. It's as though the Democrats hate SUCCESS. The Republicans give them all the HATEFUL VILE they need to hang themselves, and the Dems just ignore these open invitations to tear them a new ass. They say things like we don't want to smear people. BULLSHIT, they need to learn how to play as dirty as the republicans. The Republicans remind me of a gang, that's right, a G.A.N.G, GANG. THEY say, and DO anything. They don't care who they offend. They think it's an HONOR to be RACIST, IMMORAL, HATEFUL ,MEAN SPIRITED, IGNORANT, UNFATHFUL,(to their dumb ass wives),UNTRUTHFUL, and downright VILE

They preach a bunch of bullshit about "GOD", and Christianity to their ignorant ass followers, and ask for their vote, while they're stabbing them in the back. They depend on Racism, (and it works), and "GOD" to appeal to some of the most IGNORANT people in America. They're not as naïve as the Democrats by a long shot. The Rethugs know that HATE sells, and they use it to their advantage. Another thing that irks the shit out of me is when I hear Politicians, from both parties, talk about how smart the American people are. If the American people were smart, you wouldn't have a country divided almost 50-50 down the middle. You have one party (the republicans), that is TOTALLY, Owned, and operated by the Oil companies, the insurance companies, huge Corporations, Wall Street, Billionaires, Banks, Etc. These are all the ingredients you need to have an "Oligarchy". I don't have time to explain the definition of "Oligarchy", look it up. However, I will tell you *this, any poor, or think they're middle class person, that votes for a Republican are an IDIOT. The Republicans don't try to hide their distain and Hatred for POOR, and MIDDLE CLASS people. They openly use CLASS WARFARE, between the have Nots, (the Poor), and the "HAVE A LITTLES". (The middle class), Let me explain. They tell the "have a littles" (the alleged Middle class), that they're BETTER then the "POOR", who are blood sucking, food stamp having, unemployed, lazy, shiftless, inferior, people, who are POOR, because they WANT to be poor. They WANT to lay around all day with their big "60inch" flat screen TVs, eating bon bons ,and Lobster, bought with food stamps, and drinking expensive wine all day. Not to mention, they all buy crab legs, and JUMBO Shrimps, with their Government sponsored Welfare checks.(which there is no such thing as welfare to poor people in this country anymore, thanks to Bill Clinton) .The only WELFARE STILL in this country, is*

CORPORATE WELFARE. The Republicans openly block any help to the average working man, and openly support any and all increases to the income of these multi-Billion dollar companies, and Billionaires they love so much. If you want to rile up the Republican "Flunkies", by that I mean their 'Talking heads "like everybody on "Fox Follies", (I refuse to call that "NEWS") just say something like "raise the minimum wage". You'll have all of the Bill O'reilly and Sean Hannitys on Fox follies that same night hollering "CLASS WARFARE". I really wonder do any of their "SHEEPLE" out there in TV land, ever stop and wonder why these people who are making MILLIONS every year to LIE to them, don't want to see "REAL" hard working people make a few pennies more, and believe me, they're nothing more then a few "PENNIES". Somehow, those "SMART AMERICAN PEOPLE" that listen to this GARBAGE day in, and Day out, "VOTE FOR REPUBLICANS". It's mind baffling. How can *you vote for somebody that comes out and calls you a free loading piece of shit? You have to know that when they are talking about those "leeches in society", and those "takers", they're talking about "YOU". "OR", are you falling for the old stereotypical bullshit that all of the "TAKERS", and FREELOADERS", are them "OTHER PEOPLE",(wink, wink,) you know them NIGGERS, and Mexicans, who are trying to "TAKE OUR COUNTRY FROM US". You know who I'm talking about, "those LAZY NIGGERS that snuck into the country disguised as IMMIGRANT SLAVES in the "BOTTOM OF SLAVE SHIPS", and those diseased, IMMIGRANT MEXICANS, who keep crossing our borders illegally, even though those same borders used to belong to Mexico before we stole big hunks of their country. Now the Mexicans want to invade our country, and work for SLAVE LABOR, How dare they? It was OK when they came over and worked for almost* nothing in the fields, and the rich farmers, and corporations could make HUGE PROFITS off of their cheap labor, but now they want to "LIVE HERE"."WHAT THE FUCK? The next thing you know they'll be just like the "NIGGERS", they'll be demanding "RIGHTS", and we can't have that. SO, if you want to keep the status quo, Vote REPUBLICAN, and we'll do the rest. Don't forget, even though you're poor as hell, and don't have a pot to piss in, or a window to throw it out of, you're still better then "THEM PEOPLE". We're not going to "raise the minimum wage", or let you have unions to speak up for you, but you're still BETTER, then "them People". We're going to do everything in our power, to keep that "NIGGER IN THE WHITE HOUSE" from improving things in this country for ANYONE, including YOU, but we have to have your vote to do it. VOTE REPUBLICAN, because you're one of those SMART AMERICANS. We're going to cut as many people as we can off of FOOD

STAMPS, and deny working Americans an extension of their Unemployment checks that they worked so hard for, but we still NEED YOUR VOTE, to continue doing NOTHING FOR YOU. VOTE REPUBLICAN. We're going to continue to subsidize the Multi billion dollar a year profits of the OIL companies, who raise your prices at the gas pumps, but we still need your vote to CONTINUE DOING NOTHING FOR YOU. VOTE REPUBLICAN. We're going to do everything in our power to Destroy DEMOCRACY in this country, but we can't do it without YOU. VOTE REPUBLICAN. Now, if by chance you think you're not going to vote republican, and that you might be entertaining the thought of voting for those low life mongrels called DEMOCRATS, WE FEEL WE MUST WARN YOU THAT WE HAVE WAYS OF PREVENTING THAT TOO. It's called "VOTER SUPPRESSION". Just because you're "white" doesn't mean you can vote for whoever you want.

JAMES WITHERSPOON

We noticed that all WHITE PEOPLE didn't vote for Romney, and McCain, we still have traitors out there, and most of them live in "Blue states". Therefore, if you live in a BLUE STATE, we have a voter suppression law coming to your state too, if they're not already there. If the Republicans were to tell the truth about anything, these are the things they would have to say. However, they know this wouldn't work because even the dumbest of the dumb wouldn't fall for that. Therefore they have to use their "code words", as if the rest of us are too dumb to pick up on their "dog whistles". The Democrats however have a strange strategy, they pretend that there is no Racism, or conspiracy by the Republicans to suppress the vote, or whatever nefarious plot the republicans happen to be planning. They're sort of like Obama; they like to hide their heads in the sand. They like to say things like "OH, I like John Boehner, he's really a nice guy", "they're making him do what he's doing, it's not his fault" .BULLSHIT ,if he was such a nice guy, and had any principals he wouldn't let anybody question his principals. He's a DRUNKEN COWARD, and the Democrats all know it. Also I'd like to elaborate on that for just a little bit. If Nancy Pelosi or any Democrat for that matter were to come on public television in front of millions of people in the United States, and the world for that matter, visibly intoxicated, as john Boehner does, the Republicans would have a field day. I haven't seen NOT ONE DEMOCRAT, even mention this. Everybody laughs and makes jokes about him crying, and getting emotional when he talks about certain things in public. However, my personal opinion is he's "CRYING DRUNK," That's an old school saying, or expression about somebody who 'overindulges in alcohol, and starts crying about how much they really love their wife, or kids, or something. I'm sure most people have been around a drinker before and saw this happen. I know I have seen it happen numerous times to people I've known through the years. Hell, I've probably done it myself before in my drinking days. I know people right today who I don't like to be around when they've had "too much" to drink because I know they're going to either start crying, talking about how much they love me, or start acting Ignorant, and saying abusive things to people. Most of your bar fights are started by people like John Boehner. Remember those old beer commercials about the guy who tells his buddy, "I love you man". That's a prime example of a "crying drunk". Now, before you think I'm just being petty, let's put this into the right perspective. John Boehner and his Republican cronies want to "IMPEACH", and "SUE" Obama, FOR WHAT? Do any of those Smart Americans that "hate Obama", really think that it can be done without the whole world knowing it was done for RACIST reasons? I'm not a constitutional scholar, but I do know that the president has to have committed high crimes or treason or something very serious. The only high crime I think he has committed is letting Bush and Cheney get away scot free with murdering, and maiming thousands and Americans and Iraqis with lies. Believe me, if the shoe had been on the other foot, Obama would be facing the world court, or would have FACED the world court, and been Hung by now. LOL Sometimes I wonder if I'm the only one who thinks about things like this. For John Boehner to have the audacity to even mention impeachment in the same sentence as Obama's name, he has a lot of nerve. If anybody should be impeached it's him. Just think about it. I'll always believe that John McCain lost to Obama for being #1. A war mongering Idiot. #2. because he was old, and sick, and could die any minute, and # 3. Because he picked a nitwit for a running mate. If you looked over #1, and voted for him because you think America should be fighting somebody, somewhere, forever, you're fine. But, if you thought about the fact that #2 could have very well come into play, and he might die while president, then #3, would happen, we would've had a RACIST, NITWIT, TEABAGGER, for our president. Obviously, McCain, OR, his advisors didn't think about that, or they would have explained that to him. He must have thought there was enough Racism in the country to pull that one over on the American people. In that case, the American people really were to Smart, to fall for that. Now fast forward to today. If today, heaven forbid, something were to happen to President Obama, and Joe Biden, the Vice President, John Boehner would be next in line to be president. Some of those "Smart Americans" may not know that but it's true. For a while anyway, we would have this CRYING, DRUNKEN, COWARD as our president. ALSO, because he takes orders from the TEABAGGERS, we would probably have to listen to Dick Cheney spew his nonsense all over the airwaves again about how Obama has fucked up the Paradise him, and Bush left in Iraq. It's already sad that CNN, ABC, CBS, MEET THE

PRESS, and others already have him on the air like he's some great, old, wise, warrior, hero, but I can imagine what the fuck we would have to go through if Boehner were in charge. In other words, to make a long story short, I THINK THAT JOHN BOEHNER is a NATIONAL SECURITY RISK, and should be IMPEACHED. Maybe he can go to REHAB, or something, while he and CONGRESS are on one of their many recesses. As for his frivolous law suit against the president, that's another joke that's going to cost the American people millions of dollars for nothing. We, the people, should be suing this Republican do nothing congress, led by Boner, for theft of taxpayer money for the last 5 years. I often wonder why the Democrats are so cowardly about everything, but in a way, I know the answer, and it's not pretty either. Just because they are Democrats, doesn't mean they're really Democrats. Some of them are "DINOS" ,just like some of the republicans call their less hateful members "RINOS

".The only thing is, the Rethugs "primary" their "RINOS" if they don't HATE enough. Most of the Democrats are really down to earth, and really mean what they say. Some of them are true LIBERALS,(a dirty word nowadays),and some of them are progressives,(another dirty word).I think a lot of the Democrats that avoid being seen with Obama, or refuse to defend Obama, is because of the weakness he has shown in his negotiations, and confrontations with the Rethugs. You can't expect your followers to believe in you when you constantly show weakness in the face of the enemy, and Obama has done that over, and over, again. A lot of people make excuses for him by saying he was weak for 4 years because he was running for president again, but I personally don't buy that. I think he was weak because he believed in a lot of things the Rethugs believe in, and stand for. I've never considered him a strong "ANYTHING" to tell the truth. I've always thought of him as a moderate Republican. He just

LOVES RONALD REAGAN. Every time I hear him quote Reagan, I feel like throwing up, and I imagine a lot of Dems feel the same way. I know I was just waiting for a brave Democrat to put Sarah Palin's racist ass on the chopping block, but it never came. If the Dems would have just kept "Harping" on the Rumors about her sleeping with Glenn Rice, the black Basketball player, I don't think the tea baggers would have wanted to hear anything she had to say. They would have thrown her to the curb so quick; her head would still be spinning. Glenn Rice was just too much of a gentleman to go into details about their little sex episode. Knowing basketball players, she was probably just a piece of ass he happened to get over the weekend. However, with the Tea party being the new KKK, I don't think she would still be around calling for Obama's impeachment. That would always be in the back of their minds, when she got on stage to talk her racist bullshit. They would be thinking "I'll bet that NIGGER tore that shit up". It's a good thing I'm not a politician, I'd be a hell of a shit starter. She'd be at home playing with her guns talking to herself about death panels. She damn sure wouldn't be talking that shit she's talking now. If I was just a journalist, I'd wait until I had everybody's attention during an interview with her and ask her "do you still think about that night you spent with Glenn Rice, the Black basketball player?" that would probably be the end of my career. Anyway, I'll bet that you think I'm a Democrat by now. I don't think I am. I would rather think of myself as an independent. Obama, and the Democrats have let me down so many times, I really don't like to think of myself as a Democrat. What we really need is a true LIBERAL, OR PROGRESSIVE PARTY. We don't need another Obama, or a Democratic Party that's steadily letting it be pulled more and more to the right. At the rate we're going right now, in 20 years, we'll be kicking kids off food stamps, and yelling, and screaming

JAMES WITHERSPOON

"go home" at little immigrant kids on buses just like the republicans. The rethugs have 3 different parties in one. They have the nuts, the rightwing nuts, and the extremely nuts. Wait, make that 4 the new KKK, or tea baggers. The tea baggers control the whole thing with their HATE EVERYBODY, and EVERYTHING, philosophy. The reason I said earlier that the Republican Party reminded me of a gang is because they have a sort of initiation thing going just like some of the more notorious Gangs. In the Gangs you might have to murder, or kill somebody just to prove how heartless and cruel you are, It doesn't matter whether you know these people or not. They're just collateral damage, fuck em. Well, it's the same thing with the republicans, except the Gangs usually have rules against hurting women and kids. That's usually a serious violation to knowingly hurt either. However, the republican thugs have no such rules about hurting the weak and vulnerable. To these "COWARDS "the weaker you are, the easier it is to fuck over you. As far as they're concerned fuck you, you shouldn't be weak. It's your fault. You have to be heartless, and evil to be in their party, and somehow that makes you trustworthy, and one of them. There's no way I could be part of any organization like that and brag about it or tell anybody. Another thing that reminds me of their similarities is their worship and love of money. Gangs and drug dealers will do just about anything for money. Well guess what, so will the republicans. They'll starve you and your families to death, and at the same time, give your money to the oil companies by the Billions in "subsidies". Free money for billion Dollar companies, while children in this country starve every night. The Republican Party is a shameful organization. They have no shame about anything. In most gangs it's against the rules to pick on somebody smaller or weaker then you, you don't get any brownie points for that, you have to fight Goliath. With the republicans, they join Goliath, and help him fight YOU. However, I really do have more respect for Gangs then I do the Republican Party in other ways. I think it's unconscionable the way they treat women in general. I'll never be able to understand how a woman can bring herself to vote for a party that thinks so little of women. Over, and over, they go on, and on, about family values, and "GOD", and Christianity, and all that other good shit, then you find out they're fucking around on their wife, with somebody else's wife, and fuck God, and everybody else. The hypocrisy of these nothing ass, pieces of shit is astounding. What's so frustrating about that bullshit is the way the Democrats accept their bullshit narrative and goes along with it. They say shit like "we all know the Republican Party is the party of family values". That's a line of bullshit, and everybody knows it. They treat women like dogs, and the women that stick with them SHOULD be treated like dogs. If they like being treated that way, so be it. I would never try to change their minds. If they're that brain-dead, fuck it. You might expect that from a Homely looking, skinny, Bitch like ANN coulter, because I can imagine she has a hard time trying to get a decent man, without paying for some dick, but all republican women don't look like that. I've bedded quite a few republican women that really looked good, but they were all kind of stupid too, when it came to politics. They all seemed to have a submissive attitude. I guess they have to be, to be republicans. Anyway, a woman voting republican, is just as stupid, or self defeating as a black person, or a gay person, or even a Muslim, voting republican, or trying to join the KKK. LOL My favorite group of IDIOTS is the LOG CABIN REPUBLICANS. In case somebody out there doesn't know, or haven't heard about them, they're a group of gays that call themselves republicans. Republicans treat them like SHIT, and hate their guts. Yet, that only seems to make them want to be republicans more. They try to force themselves on the Republican Party even though they know that they hate them. I have a hard time trying to feel sorry for these dummies because I have a feeling that they HATE other Races, and other religions just like the rethugs do, but they just can't get accepted on that alone, they can't reproduce so they're shit out of luck, or S.O.L. The only people who are more nauseating then them are the Black so called Republicans like Clarence,(UNCLE TOM) Thomas. "Tom" for short and Michael Steele. They're Hilarious. Bush also had a black, cock eyed dude, as one of his advisors, who could make a maggot, gag. MSNBC used to have him on their show as some kind of republican strategist, or something, and he was hard to stomach. He put you in the mind of Alan West, That Looney tune from Florida. Totally anti Black, and ignorant as hell. I know the REAL republicans have a good old time talking about them behind their backs. If they could, I'll bet you they would join the KKK .LOL the rethugs favorite punching bag however, is the Muslims. They like to think that all Muslims are terrorists. Most rethugs couldn't tell you the difference between the Iranians, and the Iraqis, or the Shiites', and the Sunnis. All they know is they're Brown, so they must be no good MUSLIMS. They don't know, and don't care to know anything about these people other then they are "them People", and they're trying to take over this country. Another thing I don't quite understand is why we're steady giving Israel, money, bombs, and other weapons, and foreign aid that they don't need. After all the Hate and persecution that their people went through, you'd think they would be the last people on earth to kill innocent people. Yet, you see them on TV everyday bombing the hell out of women and children in a Palestinian Ghetto called the "Gaza Strip". From what I've seen on TV, that's all it is, is a strip. Yet, the United States really can't understand why these people hate this country so much. It should be self explanatory. We supply the bombs that kill their people. Obama is no better then every other President of this country that has helped murder these people. Now don't get me wrong. I don't have anything against the Jews; I just wonder how they can go from being the victims, to victimizing, and persecuting other people. I guess it's always ok as long as it isn't YOU, and YOURS. It seems to be some kind of litmus test in Congress. You have to love and support Israel. As for the Arab world, I don't particularly have a great place in my heart for them either. I found out recently that there is still a considerable amount of SLAVERY still going on in the Arab world. This is something that the whole world should be concerned about. From what I've heard on cable TV, I was under the impression that it was mostly in the "Sudan". Recently, while talking to a friend of mine from Africa, I was surprised to hear about how widespread this is. He was telling me about all of the ARAB countries where they still Own "BLACK SLAVES". I couldn't believe what I was hearing. When I think about how sorry I was feeling for some of those same Arabs in some of those countries, I got highly pissed .It just goes to show, you're never too old to learn. Now I'm wondering why we're not over there trying to help these people in the Sudan, and elsewhere who are enslaved. I'm sure Obama knows about that too. Also, why hasn't there been anything on American TV about the 200 little black school girls who were kidnapped by those black Guerilla fighters over in Africa. As usual, they talked about that for a few days, and that was it. If that had been 1 little white kid, I guarantee you OBAMA would have sent in the marines, and torn that country apart by now. Speaking of SLAVERY, The very mention of "REPARATIONS" for Blacks in America brings out all the HATE in this country. However, America has been taking Black money and giving it to Jews for Decades. What the fuck is that? America didn't exterminate the Jews Hitler and Germany did. At least Germany did the right thing and did give some form of reparations to the Jews, from what I've been told. Let me get off this dreary ass conversation, and get back to what's happening today. We now have a black president who is so hated and despised by a almost all white, Racist, republican Congress, that they have basically shut all progress down in this country for the last five years. They have hurt so many of the American people, trying to get back at Obama, that I think they should all be tried as criminals, for treason. They have systematically stopped this country dead in its tracks, and prevented it from moving forward. This was all planned the very same night that Obama was inaugurated as president of this country. Jew boy Cantor, Mitch McConnell, Paul Ryan, and all the usual suspects should have been bought up on charges of treason by now. We all know that Obama would never have the guts to ruffle any feathers about something like that. A lot of the problems that Obama is experiencing right today is because of his lack of courage. From all of the criminals who shout about Benghazi, to the piece of SHIT that hollered out "you lie", while he was making a speech. This would have all been prevented if he had just stood up like a man. He has been so busy trying not to be an "Angry Black Man", that he doesn't appear to be a "MAN", at all. The rethugs smell this FEAR, and WEAKNESS, and move in for the KILL like the RATS that they are. A lot of people think that Obama has finally found a backbone because he has lately been calling out the rethugs for being a bunch of obstructionist assholes, but all of this might be too little, too late. They have already done their damage, and branded him as a "Coward", A lawless, dictator, a wannabe King, and a tyrant. At the same time, they have called him "weak, and ineffective", lazy, a monarch, you name it. Frankly I've never heard of a "WEAK" dictator, or Tyrant. My opinion is that if you called a dictator "weak", you would probably be dead by now. You can't have it both *ways. They know that the intelligent people in America think they're a bunch of IDIOTS, and want them gone. However, they don't CARE, what the intelligent people think. They care about what the TEABAGGERS THINK, and what the KKK thinks, and what a Drug addicted, ignorant racist, fat piece of shit named Rush thinks. (Rush stands for the highs he gets from condemning Obama). My thought is that if these are the people that you consider your leaders, or your base, you are no better then them. Like the old saying goes, "birds of a feather, flock together," Therefore the Democrats need to get off that "BULLSHIT ",about Boehner being a "nice Guy being forced to fuck over the entire country by a small band of tea baggers", especially the black Congressmen, and spokespeople. You would think by now that they would be able to spot a uncover racist, and bigot. Let's get this straight, ain't nobody making Boehner do nothing he don't want to do, so quit making up excuses for him. Giving him the benefit* of the doubt is useless, stupid, and counter productive to your common sense. Everything you hear coming out of his DRUNKEN MOUTH, is his own, and real opinion. Nobody is forcing him to do anything. I also stand by my assertion that he is a "NATIONAL SECURITY RISK", to this country, and should be treated as such. Have you noticed how every now and then, "Boner" has an "INTELLIGENT ATTACK"? By that, I mean he says something that the republicans don't want to hear. He sometimes tells the truth. Then the next day he has to go back and "clarify" what he said, and what he "really meant "It's quite obvious that they jumped all over his ass ,and made him repent for the sin of telling the "truth."They probably tell him " we know you were Drunk, and didn't really mean what you said", so tomorrow say this, or that, and we'll forgive you. Now do we really need a puppet like that, or someone that can't think a clear thought on his own without being told to take it back. I don't think he needs to be anywhere near being next in line to be P.O.T.U.S. However, there's one thing you have to give the Republicans credit for. They are MASTERS at brainwashing people into voting against themselves, and their own best interests. They also know how to use the "HATE" in their base to get votes. What's so shameful about this is that the Democrats are so cowardly, they're afraid to call them out on that fact. When the Democrats see the republican thugs out there protesting, and holding up ignorant ass, racist ass signs about OBAMA, they start making up excuses for these peoples behavior. They say things like, "oh, that's just a small fringe group of people". That's "bullshit, and they know it. The truth is, "That small fringe group of people "is about 49% of the country. That's right, 49% of this country are RACIST IDIOTS. The Democrats know that if they make too big of a deal about it, the next day, Fox Follies will be all over TV, telling their empty headed, racist ass viewers, that the Democrats called ALL republicans RACISTS, and IDIOTS, and stupid motherfuckers, even though it's true. I don't understand this because none of these people are going to vote for them anyway. They might as well say what the fuck they really, and truly think, people who vote republican, are some DUMB ASS, RACIST, Ignorant, motherfuckers .Facts are facts. The republicans have no problem calling Democratic supporters names. They even call people who won't talk bad about Obama, and the Democrats, names. With the republicans, you're either "with" them or against them. That's why I say they remind me of a GANG. With them there is no "middle ground". If you don't "HATE OBAMA", you're the enemy, plain and simple. I often wondered how the republican spin machine could have people out protesting,(the tea baggers),AKA ,the KKK, holding up totally, meaningless, brain-dead, signs, like "keep your Government hands off my Social Security, and my Medicare". It seemed to me that "Somebody", "somewhere", standing next to one of these IDIOTS, would say,"Hey man, that sign makes no sense, the Government is the one that gives you your social Security check, and your Medicare". Yet, not one reporter, from any station, including MSNBC, ever had the nerve, or the courage to bring this to people's attention. NOT ONE. I think I figured it out. The Democrats as usual, are too cowardly, and chickenshit to bring it up because they don't want to offend the republican base, and the republicans don't give a shit, because they know that the majority of their base is a bunch of uneducated, ignorant, racist, old ass white people, who can't stand the idea of a Black man being in the White House. That's where you get your chant, "We're going to take our country back". These old, racist ass white people never thought they would see the day that a Black Man would be the President of the United States, and they HATE IT with a passion. In their eyes, this is what happens when you "let them "Niggers" get an education". They get "uppity" and think they're as smart as white people. They feel that these new, LIBERAL, white people are weak, and destroying everything they've ever worked for. They don't just hate Obama, and the entire Black race, they hate the LIBERAL WHITE PEOPLE TOO, namely the Democrats. Imagine, trying to explain to your kids that all the lies you told your kids about Black people being inferior to them, exploding in your face. After all, to feel superior to everybody else in the world, you have to be able to look down on them.Everytime they see Obama on TV; it's a reminder to them, of their failure. Don't think for a minute that this only applies to Old, half dead white people; this also applies to a lot of middleclass people who don't even know they're racist yet. It's no accident that the hate groups have tripled in number since Obama became president, it was bound to happen. America's racism just exploded. One thing I like about Mitt Romney is that he had so much confidence in American racism, that he thought that he could say anything about "POOR PEOPLE", and get away with it. What he didn't realize was that republican policies had hurt and shrunk the middleclass down to almost nothing. The Bush years did more damage to the middleclass, and the country in general then any time in recent history. Keep in mind the middleclass has always been made up mostly of white people, not blacks, or any other race. Therefore, whites were hurt more then anybody just by the sheer numbers alone. Sure, Blacks were hurt more in areas of unemployment,, but Black people are used to being the last hired, but first fired all of our lives. This is nothing new to Black people, or Mexicans and other races too. White people aren't used to being unemployed, if they want a job, they just go get a job. When Romney's use of his usual "code words", were made public, his code words like "Givers"(white people),and "takers" "(black people),what he failed to understand was that he included millions of newly unemployed whites in that category, too ,not just those "other people". When he talked about people wanting someone to take care of them, he didn't seem to realize that white people "Always" receive more from social programs then Blacks, or anybody else. Social Security, Medicare, Medicaid, Food stamps, V A benefits, you name it. White people make up the bulk of all of these programs. He was so out of touch with "regular people", that he didn't realize what the fuck he was saying. The people he included as "takers "were senior citizens, (most of them white), unemployed people, (most of them white), wounded soldiers from the republican wars, (most of them white), Kids on food stamps, (most of them white, soldiers on food stamps, (most of them white). I could go on, and on, but that subject alone could be a whole separate book. What Romney thought was that he could depend on MOST of the white people in the country being STUPID enough to think that it was a "white givers" VS "Black Takers "election, and that this BLACK MAN, in the White House was giving all of the white peoples money to Black people. When in reality, anybody with half a brain could see that Obama wasn't then, and still isn't today, thinking about doing anything for anybody black. He was scared shitless that the republicans would say he was trying to help Black people if he even said the word "POOR". Right to today, Obama won't say "POOR". Obama even uses "code words", just like the republicans. His favorite "code word "is "MIDDLECLASS." Black people need to realize that "middleclass" does not mean them. This word helps him assure white people that he's not trying to do "ANYTHING", for any Black people, but he's looking out for the "white middleclass". Obama has made it abundantly clear that the only thing he's going to do for the Black community is preach, and browbeat the Black MEN in the community, about being better fathers, with NOTHING to work with. Bill Cosby does the same thing, but I can see where he's coming from. Bill has donated hundreds of millions of dollars to the United Negro College and he don't give a fuck about the white establishment knowing he's trying to help his people. I can see why Romney thought this might work because it had worked for the republicans so many times before, and there was no reason to think it wouldn't work again. He already knew that the racial hatred in the country was at an all time high because we had elected a Black President, and he wanted to capitalize on it. He also thought that now was his best chance, if he ever would have a chance, because he also knew that a lot of people didn't particularly like him because he was known to outsource jobs, kill jobs for his own personal wealth, didn't give a fuck about anybody but the rich, and so on. What he didn't know was that his remark about the 47% being loafers and "takers "resonated with a lot of white people who knew in their hearts he was really only out for the rich, and "Super Rich", and that didn't include them. Not to mention everybody knew he was a tax cheat. I think that really hurt him, because people wonder why you have to cheat on your taxes, when you're a Billionaire. Maybe he really thought that most white people were rich or something, I don't know. Either way it went, that was a dumb thing to say. I think a lot of people are beginning to realize that this country is on the road to becoming a complete Oligarchy, or plutocracy. People are beginning to realize that at the pace we are going they are not going to have a place in that atmosphere. Without the middleclass, there will only be rich, and poor, not many choices are there. I think the country really dodged a bullet, by not electing Mitt Romney for president. I truly believe he would have taken this country back 100 years to the days of the robber barons. While he was running for president, the republicans did everything they could to keep anybody from bringing up his college days when he dressed up like a cop, and stopped people on the highway pretending he was a real cop. There is no telling how many women he sexually assaulted, or harassed during those years. He was a carbon copy of Bush in his younger days. A spoiled rich brat taking advantage of his family power and wealth. For some reason, the American people seem to like electing rich people to higher office. Rich people who have nothing in common with them whatsoever. However, I can see why that won't change anytime in the near or far future for that matter. Because the people making the laws will not change that, never will. I hope anyone reading this don't think I'm being over critical of Obama, because I know how Black people have a tendency to think about black people criticizing other black people in public. Especially powerful Black people. We tend to be just as clannish as white people. I would automatically jump to Obama's defense if I hear a white person criticize him. I guess that's just the nature of the beast. I know that because, I've done it. It's just like you talking about your kid, but you don't want another motherfucker talking about him, or her. I would listen to friends of mine talk about their wives, but I would never say a word. The main reason I would just listen was because I knew that when they came to their senses they would say why did you talk bad about my old lady? It's a matter of knowing when the fuck to just shut the fuck up. As much as I try, I can't get my mind off of all those young black kids sitting up in jail for non violent weed smoking charges. I guess Obama's not going to do anything unless the whole country legalizes weed. Just think if you were in Jail, doing time for something that everybody outside, is doing, and it's legal now? That would piss me off to the high heavens. A lot of you people who think I'm angry at Obama are going to be in for a surprise. Wait until those kids sitting in jail all of this time Obama's been president, get out. Then you're going to hear some real anger If I sound angry, it's because I am. I don't like the idea that Obama can go to sleep at night and not think about all the young black kids victimized by these cruel, idiotic laws. I remember when I was the victim of White on black crime. We always talk about Black on black crime, but we never talk about white on black crime. I look at all of the white on black crime today, and I have finally figured it out. We're not "supposed to talk about white on black crime, and it happens everyday, all over this country. The republicans, have Obama where they want him, "Afraid of his own shadow" .They have really "WON". By that I mean they've accomplished what they wanted by neutralizing him. Even though they say a lot if Idiotic things like he's an illegal alien, and not from this country, and he has committed all kinds of crimes against the Constitution of the United States, and should be Impeached, and sued, and all of the other nonsense they talk. They know none of this makes sense. All of the made up, so called SCANDALS are just that "MADE UP." What they have done is "made sure "that there won't be "Another" Black President". They don't care that they make themselves look foolish, and inept, as long as they accomplish their goal. They don't give a flying fuck about the inequality that exists in this country, or the people that they hurt. It's all about themselves, and their all consuming Ideology. As far as they're concerned "Fuck the American People", and that's exactly what they've done, and are still doing. This isn't going to stop until Obama is out of office. An example of their persistence is "Fox Follies. Everybody knows this isn't a real news station. Some of the things they say are down right laughable. They'll say things like the president is laughing on TV, and "no president has EVER LAUGHED ON TV". They don't think he should "EVER "take a day off. He shouldn't take a "SHIT", while the country is burning to the ground". He shouldn't "talk" a certain way, he shouldn't "walk" a certain way, He shouldn't "BOW", a certain way because Bush, would never BOW to Japan or China. "HORRORS, "He even put his foot up on the top of the Desk in the Oval office. I'll bet every president since Lincoln, and George Washington has FUCKED on top of that desk. Anyway, they mainly say all of these unbelievable, just plain stupid things because nobody ever questions them on anything; they just print it, or report it. Everything these Idiots say can be proven false, but we have a Media that helps them mislead the public, over, and over, again. It's almost sickening to watch "Meet the press". They seem to belong to the Republican Party. They're no better then Fox Follies. You can't take them serious either. They used to be pretty "Fair and balanced". Now, they're just a republican Parrot station. They trot out some of the most "outrageous", and "Idiotic "of the LOONEY TUNES. I don't know who they think wants to hear from "WAR CRIMINAL" DICKHEAD CHENEY? Who wants to hear from McCain, and Romney, "Both" of the sore losers that Obama defeated. The news media "LOOKS" for these people because they "WANT" to hear all the "hate", and vitriol coming out of these peoples mouths. Bush and Cheney left office in Disgrace, and should be the last people anybody wants to hear from on TV everyday, or any day for that matter. At least bush is somewhere painting pictures of his Toes, and the back of his head. LOL Cheney Likes to keep getting on TV and keep reminding the families of the Dead, and Maimed soldiers, that if he had the chance, he would send them back over there, and get them KILLED and MAIMED again. Cheney doesn't even think about all of the Men, Women, and CHILDREN his regime "MURDERED "in IRAQ.(At last count, an estimated 160,000 people .Yet, in spite of that fact, somebody, somewhere, in a high place of authority, saw it fit and proper to give this old "living piece of shit ",a new heart, ahead of thousands of dying young people, who needed a heart. A waste of a perfectly good heart. Yet, it's not really him that's so disturbing, it's the silly motherfuckers who still support him, and don't see where he did anything wrong. And you're going to tell me there's No such thing as CLASS WARFARE? If the RICH people in this country like Cheney had their way, we'd have a country full of OLD ASS, MOTHERFUCKING, Vampire, rich people sporting young people's hearts. And guess what? The Republican Party would still be conning the same stupid, ass fuckers that vote for them today, into voting against themselves again. Like the saying goes, "the definition of insanity is doing the same thing over, and over, again, but expecting a different result. So much for Cheney. I guess you've figured out by now that I'm not just angry at Obama; I'm "Mad" at the whole political system in this country. The republicans are easy to dislike. No fuck that, I HATE the Republican Party. I hate them because they're so hateful, and mean that you don't feel bad about hating them. You know they deserve it. They "Hate""everybody, and everything". They hate Women, Kids ,Japs ,Jews ,Sex, marijuana,

Black people, Brown people, Red people, yellow people , Gays, lesbians, transgender people, you name it, they Hate it. They even hate some White people. (DEMOCRATS).Like everything though, there are 2 sides to every story. They are fond of a few things they love Money, War, GUNS, cheating on their wives, being gay, but not admitting it, lying etc. I'm not going to put "GOD" down as one of the things they love because that would be a lie. They also have a strange love for "WAR". You see you would think they were all soldiers. Not true. I'm talking about Republican politicians now, not just the poor ass people that vote for them. The republican politicians love War and money because they profit from war and make money from it. They don't like "FIGHTING WARS THEMSELVES" they like sending other people to war for them. They do everything they can "NOT "to be in a war zone. They don't want "Their Kids" in war, they want to send "your Kids" into war. They love getting in front of the cameras, and talking tough. When they're talking about they LOVE "GUNS, "they mean BUY more guns, because they're all bought and paid for, as lobbyists for the NRA .Most of them motherfuckers probably couldn't hit the side of a barn if you paid them. They also have contracts with the gun manufacturers ,so they need to have somebody to kill. It's called war profiteering. As for "God", that's a bad joke. These people don't believe in God. They use God against the people that do believe. God and war in the same sentence is an oxymoron. How could these warmongers be religious? They take advantage of the ignorance of the church crowd. Haven't you ever wondered how they pull that off? They talk about god all the time, and yet they Hate everybody, and everything. I think they know that you can't be TOO smart when you believe that there's an invisible man watching over you night and day. You tell stories like that to your "kids", not adults. It's too bad the religious nuts don't like to read nothing but the BIBLE, otherwise, they might have read about how Bush was talking about how naive, and gullible church people are. He had a special team in the white house just for Bullshitting the church people. Bush also made up his Texas accent for the stupid asses who wanted to believe he was from Texas. I think he's originally from back east somewhere like Connecticut. He played that game so long that now he really thinks he is from Texas. The Democrats on the other hand have their Hearts in the right place, but they just don't know how to do shit right. They're the goody 2 shoe party who likes to do everything by the book. The Democrats remind you of a nerdy homebody kid trying to tell a street savvy kid how to make it in the streets. It can't be done. The republicans rig the game constantly and keep the Democrats wondering what the fuck they just did. The Democrats are usually left trying to figure out what scheme the republicans are dreaming up next. This is the reason the Dems frustrate their base so much. You see the republicans knew that Nancy Pelosi was automatically NOT going to do any IMPEACHING, or starting any unnecessary fights with the republicans because #1 She's a woman #2she's a liberal, and not an evil bitch like most of the women in their party. #3 they figured that she would influence Obama to let bygones be bygones, and they were right.(Of course I don't think for a minute, that it took much to make him agree, to not do anything, to anybody). Not that I'm excusing Obama for being weak and spineless, it's just in his nature to go along to get along. the republicans view women as fickle and weak. That's why they don't have many women in high positions in their party. It's a no brainer. There are probably a lot of plans and things they meet about and never even discuss with the women in their party until they need their rubberstamp vote. They only use them when they need them. Just like a lot of men think about their wives. "Shut up and be quiet until I need some "SEX".I guess that's ok, if you can find someone stupid enough, and with a total lack of self esteem, to go along with it. Personally, I don't gravitate toward women who let me just fuck over them. There's no challenge there. To each his own, I guess. I'm going to name this book something that is going to be eye grabbing, yet not exactly what it seems. However, don't get me wrong, I'm not trying to mislead anyone, (If I did that I wouldn't be any better then a rethugligan)I just mostly want to turn peoples Hate against them. That has a sort of irony to it. By the time they realize that I don't really HATE OBAMA, they'll be half way through the book. Plus, I really DO think that Obama made a BIG mistake by not prosecuting Bush, and Cheney, for war crimes. That is going to forever be a stain on his presidency, and will forever baffle historians 100 years from now. By the same logic though, Historians are probably not going to be too kind to the racist obstructionism perpetrated by this republican Congress either. The republican Congress has done everything in their power to try to hurt Obama's presidency, and it's all too obvious. There's nothing they can do to sugar coat their Hatred of Obama. You can't compare Obama's problems to any other Democratic president. As much as they Hated Clinton, and did everything they could to damage his presidency, it still doesn't compare because it wasn't done out of racism. However, sometimes you can overdo things and complain too much. I think people are beginning to realize that the republicans are making too much out of everything Obama does. Anything and everything is Obama's fault, no matter how serious, or how trivial it is. The really ridiculous part of this hypocrisy is that it's usually something that every other president in history has done. They want to complain about such nonsense and petty bullshit as how many times he plays golf, or is the taxpayer paying for him to have special people walking his dog. Who in their right mind would even think of such bullshit, and nonsense? I'll tell you who, dumbass Sarah Palin, and dipshit Michelle Bachmann, that's who. That's not unusual however. What's unusual is that it's big news on Fox Follies, the Racist RAG that calls itself a news station. It's amazing that that piece of journalistic shit is still in circulation. The fact of the matter is that if Obama was White, I don't think they would still be in business. Only in America could you have a FOREIGNER, from another country, come into this country, and try to Destroy one of it's major political parties, and the POTUS with made up proven lies, and innuendoes. The reason that is possible is because the owner of Fox follies is immune from prosecution because he's super Rich, and in this country, that's all you have to be , you can get away with Murder ,fraud, theft, rape, and anything else, as long as you have money. If Rupert Murdock was in a lot of countries, he would be in jail, as would most of our politicians. Only in America can you steal

BILLONS, and pay back just millions of dollars in fines, out of the money you stole. President Obama, Eric Holder, and the entire U.S government should be facing charges right today for this travesty of the law. I'm not joking when I say things like that because in those cases, Obama is no better then Bush, and Cheney. Before I forget, there another thing that bugs me about Obama. While everybody in the country is losing wages, and bleeding money out of both pockets, Wall Street, and the big corporations are doing just GREAT. The stock market is at an all time high, the banks are still too big to fail, or Jail. After robbing the American people out of their homes and money. Not 1 person has been walked out of Wall Street in cuffs, and the band plays on. All of you people that have a habit of looking the other way when it comes to Obama need to wake up. If the republicans were really serious about "impeaching", they would probably have a REAL CASE, if they went that route. However, they have no interest in the *prosecuting anybody for stealing the average working mans money because they're on these thieves payroll. They are the ones, (right along with Obama), who make all of this possible. Black unemployment has doubled under Obama, yet Black people defend and support him to the bitter end. Obama's home town Chicago, or CHIRAQ as I call it, is a war zone. Black people ignore that as if it doesn't exist. Black people supported that asshole Rahm Emanuel because he was one of Obama's best friends, and advisors. "Thanks OBAMA," for endorsing and giving us that piece of shit for Mayor. He worked with Obama long enough to get well known by the Black People of Chicago, then Quit the White House, and immediately went straight back to Chicago and ran for Mayor. That was a plan that worked to a "T". That was his plan all the time, and Obama knew it. His connections to Obama made him a shoo in with the Black voters. They could have easily elected a black Mayor had it not been for Obama.*

Wake up Black People. The first thing Emanuel did when he took office was started shutting down schools in the Black neighborhoods. Thanks Obama. This doesn't necessarily mean that Obama knew he was going to do that, but after he did, it seems that Obama would have had a meeting with him, and asked him "what the fuck are you doing? Hey, wait a minute, I'm trying to tell other people not to fall for Obama's Bullshit, and here I am making up excuses for him myself, and Lying to myself at the same time. Of course Obama knew what Rahm was going to do. Obama didn't want to be in Chicago when Rahm made his move because he knew Rahm was a conservative Democrat, and would start chopping on the black neighborhoods few resources as soon as he got in Office. Plus, Rahm didn't want to wait until Obama served both of his terms. I could go on and on about Obama's total lack of interest in Black people, and their problems, but I think you get the point by now. I think that Part of that lack of interest comes from the fact that he knows he has, or "HAD" our vote locked up, and didn't have to court us like he did the Hispanic vote. In other words, he took us for granted, and still does. We've given him a blank check as far as where our loyalty lies. As much as I love Al Sharpton, (he really believes what he says most of the time), I get really aggravated when I see him on MSNBC harping about how "Obama, really slammed the republican party when he said so and so". I've never heard Obama "really slam" any republican. Before his re election, he wouldn't even say the word "republican". He avoided that word as much as he avoided the word "POOR", and he still refuses to say "poor' even today. When he wants to say something about "poor People", he has Joe Biden say it. Now when it come to Hispanics, that's a different story. Obama fights tooth and nail for the Hispanics. Everybody knows the Hispanics overwhelmingly voted for Obama and Democrats in general, that's no secret. That's why the rethugs are against Immigration so wickedly .They consider every new Hispanic that comes into the country as a new DEM vote, and they might be right, after all the it's not like many of them are going to vote republican. after all of the bullshit they continue on a daily basis to put them through. Now don't get me wrong, I don't harbor any ill feelings toward Mexicans or any other kind of Immigrant. I have a couple of kids by a Mexican Woman myself. She was born and raised in Chicago, but she's still Mexican. After all, we're all sort of in the same boat. However, it gets my goat when I hear the Mexican, or Hispanic representatives threatening Obama about how much he owes the Hispanics for their vote, and support. There's nothing wrong with that, however, they have to get in line just like Black people. They seem to think he owes more to them then he does to his own people, and for good reason. They're afraid he's going to forget about them like he's forgotten about Black People. This is not their fault, its Black peoples fault for blindly following Obama, and never demanding anything in return. The last time I checked, I think Obama won something like 70% of the Hispanic vote. It was more like 93% of the Black vote, so who does he owe the most? Yes, there are still some Hispanics out there voting against themselves, mostly the ones who came to this country legally. My kids mother of Mexican descent, was one of those Mexicans who seemed to dislike the Mexicans who came over here Illegally. She called them BRAZZERS. I don't even know what the hell that means. I asked her one time, and she gave me some kind of bullshit answer about how BRAZZERS dressed in loud, colorful clothes or something. I didn't know what the fuck she was talking about. But as far as who we get to vote for, It's not like either of us have much of a choice, its DEMS, or nobody. Yet, nowadays, it's Immigration this, or immigration that. It's always at the forefront of the issues, and mainly because the Hispanics keep it in the forefront. The united Black caucus needs to get off their asses and DEMAND SOMETHING, instead of following Obama around blindly, and waiting on him to do something that he's never going to do. At least he's not going to do anything as long as he's in Office anyway. He might turn into an activist once he leaves office, but I don't really seeing him ruffling too many feathers as long as the republicans control Congress. In the meantime, the only thing Blacks get from Obama is Lectures about fatherhood. You can't be a good father without MONEY; I don't care how much you love your kids, this is a fact, it's not fantasy. At the present time Obama is asking for BILLIONS of dollars to help Hispanic youths coming into the country illegally. Why can't he summon up enough courage to ask for BILLIONS of dollars to help the "POOR" Black kids who are already here? The same poor, Black Men, Women, And yes kids, who have been working minimum wage jobs, and *paying taxes out of those piece of shit jobs to bring people from other countries here. Yes, we were immigrants once upon a time too, hundreds of years ago, but we didn't break into this country illegally, they, (white folks), did us the honor of coming to our country, and picking us up. They wanted us really bad, only they didn't want to pay us minimum wage, they didn't PAY US ANYTHING. We didn't jump fences, swim across the Rio Grande, walk through 60 or 70 miles of desert, or come in the trunks of cars. We didn't pay coyotes thousands of dollars to bring us here.(I've always wondered where they got thousands of Dollars to pay coyotes?).I thought they were supposed to be so ("poor").Hell, I know a bunch of Black people who have been here all of their lives, and don't have thousands of dollars to give anybody for anything. We came in the bottom of ships forcibly, not by choice. Yes, SLAVERY, the ugliest word in the human language. The word white people hate to hear. The word that describes* the horrors that their ancestors inflicted on a whole race of people for hundreds of years. The word that makes most White people squeamish around Black people. The word that makes white people afraid of Black people. Yet, these very same people have the nerve to call these very same people that they worked until they died, LAZY. Black people have always been their victims, and continue to this very day to be their victims, yet, most white people today have the nerve to think that black people are Lazy. Why because of ignorance. Most prejudices come from ignorance. If you look at the way the Republicans in Congress treat Obama you'll see why I brought this up. They call him the "food stamp president". This is a direct slur against black people, and OBAMA, and they mean for HIM, and US, to get the message. They go out of their way to send a message to the entire black population of this country. That message is "we don't intend to "ever" let up on your race, whether you have a black man for president or not. That message is: Don't think of Obama as your "HERO", because as far as we're concerned, he's still a "NIGGER", with a capital "N". Their message is, "don't get up too much hope", because you see the way we treat your Hero with no respect don't you? SEE, right there is where I get all fucked up in the head. I know what you're going to say, that is, "he can't say certain things because he's the president; they treat ALL presidents that way". NO, that's not true, and you know it's not true. I've never heard the republicans say anything about Bill Clinton's birth certificate, or where he came from? The republicans have never stood up while Clinton was giving a speech in the halls of Congress, and called him a "liar". You've never heard them call him a "Redneck from Arkansas" or anything like that. If they had, you can bet, Clinton would have said something like, yeah, "but this redneck beat your ass at the polls didn't he"? Like I was saying at the beginning of this book, Bullies pick, and choose who they're going to fuck with. Obama's a lot different. The next day after one of them has insulted him, you might see Obama "Skinnin and "grinnin" with that same asshole as if nothing has happened. I know Obama may not be able to come out and say "I'll beat your Motherfucking ass pussy", but he could at least show "anger", by that I mean EXTREME ANGER. You could do that without passing a blow. Obama is an extremely intelligent man, and they all know it .I don't think I've seen not one of these idiots who I thought was smarter, or even half as smart as Obama .However, they have his number because they know he's trying to avoid the "angry black man" stereotype, so they take advantage of it. Don't think for a moment that a lot of Dems don't want him to fight back, a lot of them would be more then happy to see OBAMA display a pulse. In my job, I come in contact with a lot of White people, who feel the same way. They say things like, "I thought Obama would be a bad motherfucker when he got in Office, but he sure let me down". I don't know if they're saying things like that because I'm black, or if they are kind of apologizing for the way they see him being treated by other white people. Either way, it let's me know that I'm not being oversensitive, or imagining things. It goes to show you that not ALL white people are racist Idiots like the Republican Party, and there are a lot of good people in this world regardless of race. Lately they've been using another little game they play with him. They keep calling him "Weak and ineffective". They're hoping he'll make the mistake of trying to prove them wrong. Some shit just went down in Russia where an Airplane was shot down, and over 200 people were killed. Now the republican bullies want Obama to start talking big shit to Putin. This is a dangerous game they are playing. They want Obama to go out on a limb, and start threatening Russia with some kind of retaliation. We're talking about threatening a country with big time nuclear weapons. We're not talking about one of those little weak countries the United States has a habit of bullying around. This isn't Iraq, or Grenada, Afghanistan, or Viet Nam. As soon as Obama takes the bait; they're going to say "this is Obama's Iraq." In the meantime, they're trying to instigate him into starting the cold War all over again, so that they can have it on record that he started a war just like Bush. Then, they'll promptly say now you can't talk about "Bush", look a democrat started a war this time". As always, the leader of this "bomb, bomb, bomb, everybody" bullshit is John"chickenhawk" McCain. John McCain is the leader in all of this bullshit, and Lindsey Graham is his little parrot, and effeminate partner, who has never seen a war he didn't want to send your kids off too in the name of "BIG OIL". Lindsey Graham, who looks like he couldn't "fight his way out of a paper bag". I'll never figure out "HOW" ", or "WHY" John McCain is considered a HERO in everybody's eyesight. All the fuck he ever did during the Viet Nam war was get "shot the fuck down". Any fucking dummy can do that, what's the big fucking deal about him being a hero. After all, he hadn't shot down 10 or 11 enemy planes before he was shot down. He wasn't the "RED BARON" or anybody. How many enemy planes did he shoot down. My guess is NONE, ZIP, ZERO. As a matter of fact, nobody likes to talk about the fact that he was responsible for some other people dying aboard an aircraft carrier trying to save his useless ass life, after he virtually destroyed a perfectly good Jet plane. He was really only another spoiled brat, Who happened to be the son of an Admiral? I guess that means he automatically gets anointed "HERO, by Birth" status. Bullshit, He was a PRISONER, plain and simple, nothing else. He was a P.O.W, prisoner of war. Prisoners of war are not HEROES. They're captured men. What's so HEROIC about that? Are we really that desperate for an American Hero? I guess we are They all simply ignore the stories about him co operating with the Viet Cong ,and doing everything in his power to keep anybody from coming home from the concentration camps, after he was released. He stopped the Americans from trying to find, and bring home anymore MIAs. No need to ask What the fuck that was all about because we know what it was all about. It was about nobody coming home from the Hanoi Hilton and telling what happened over there.. Well fuck McCain, back to Obama. Well, it's kind of scary knowing Obama's track record, for trying to do everything in his power, to make the republicans like him. I just hope he doesn't do anything stupid. By stupid, I mean like letting the neo cons that hate his guts, goad him into starting the COLD War all over again, or even possibly, a NUCLEAR WAR. "Now wouldn't that be a kick in the balls? Just think, the headlines on "False News" before we were all evaporated, would be: "BLACK PRESIDENT DESTROYS WORLD, I TOLD YOU WE SHOULD HAVE IMPEACHED

HIM FIRST". Republicans would love that. Their plan is to harass Obama into doing something they know the American people are tired of, and that's confronting other countries all over the world about things that are none of our business. I'm sure Obama is going to weigh in on that American Palestinian youth who was beaten by Israeli soldiers. It was all caught on camera. The young kid was all bruised up, and had 2 black eyes. However, that kid didn't have to go to the Gaza strip to be beaten up. He could have stayed right here in the United States and the same thing could have happened, and he wouldn't have to be caught throwing rocks, at soldiers or policemen. You see, in the United States, We, (Black PEOPLE), are the Palestinians in the Gaza strip. The Racist white cops in the United States are the brutal Israelis killing and beating Black people. (When we're not killing each other). We have a lot in common. The Black neighborhoods in the United States have long been "Occupied" by white, Racist, and "Uncle Tom" (Black) cops. Just in the last week, a white cop was caught on people's cell phone cameras beating an older Black lady unmercifully on a public Highway for walking down the shoulder of the highway.(what a horrible crime), This woman was obviously having mental problems. This "COWARDLY" piece of shit was probably beating somebody's Grandmother to a pulp. For this assault on this poor lady, he was "REWARDED" with a desk job with pay, while they do an investigation that will surely "clear" him of all charges. I'm sure he'll say he was in fear for his life,(which are the MAGIC words today), while he was beating the shit out of her, and no charges will be filed. I hope I'm wrong, but that's the usual pattern. Then yesterday, a "GANG" of cops "MURDERED", a 350 lb Black man for the outrageous crime of "suspicion of selling loose cigarettes". They "attacked, and choked him to death". I guess they were worried about him stealing profits from the cigarette companies. Yet, as of this writing Obama, and Eric Holder, and his INJUSTICE dept, have said absolutely "NOTHING". My guess is that they(the cops), will go on "VACATION WITH PAY", until they find out that all of those "brave cops were in fear for their lives while they were "choking him to death". These are some of the reasons "Obama should be IMPEACHED". The republicans are "making up" reasons to Impeach Obama, when in reality, they do have some real reasons to Impeach him, and Eric Holder Too. Again, I know that some black people will be upset by some of the things I'm saying, but they're true. I'm NOT a politician, nor do I claim to be one, but what I do is "WATCH" politicians, and what they DO, and DON"T DO. Obama needs to be impeached for a lot of things he "doesn't do". Here's just a short list of things he doesn't do, or didn't do. # 1. He refused to uphold the law. And charge Bush, and Cheney with MASS MURDER. #2.He didn't charge Bush and Cheney with torture, which they openly admit too, and Cheney openly brags about on "face the Nation", and FOX FOLLIES, his favorite propaganda stations. Plus, Cheney even goes so far as to say, Obama is a "weakling" because he won't continue with what he, (Cheney) started. That's the kind of appreciation, and thanks, Cheney gives to the man who let him get away with "MASS MURDER, AND TORTURE", president Obama. Why don't the republicans IMPEACH OBAMA FOR THAT? That would be something that any republican or Democratic attorney would have a good chance with, as far as impeachment is concerned. The republicans don't have to "Fabricate "shit" ,they have some real shit right in front of their faces. #3.IMPEACH OBAMA, and ERIC HOLDER, for "NOT DOING ANYTHING" to the WALL STREET CRIMINALS". These criminals freely "STOLE" the American people's money, and homes, at will, and continue to this very day to steal money, and not one thing is being done about it other then those "weak ass fines" That Eric Holder's injustice dept dishes out. Meanwhile, business goes on as usual for the "WALL SREET CRIMINALS". Actually, that's not true, business has "Zoomed to "record breaking levels" since Obama has been in office. "Wall Street should LOVE OBAMA" if anything, not despise him like they do. They "LOVED" the Bush administration when they helped them Rob the American people blind with his tax cuts for the rich.. I guess they can't stand the Idea that a "BLACK MAN" helped them to make all the Billions of dollars that they currently make on the backs of the poor, and middle class, people of this country. There's just no honor among thieves anymore. Anyway, moving right along. #4.The "too big to fail banks" have grown bigger, and will never have to worry about failing as long as Obama is in office. They're doing great, as the rest of the country works for less, and income inequality increases. The Billionaires have never been in better shape, and couldn't be happier.

JAMES WITHERSPOON

They can continue to buy our Politicians, (some Democrats included), and our Democracy, and continue on the road to making this country a complete OLIGARTY, and plutocracy. The Koch's, the Walton's, (of Wal-Mart fame) and other Billionaires like Sheldon Addelson, can continue to bid on all of our republican politicians, and some of our Democratic ones as well. They have private auctions at expensive resorts where they do all their bidding. They even have these private auctions where they invite and purchase all of our "Republican conservative Supreme court Justices". It's tragic that the people in this country have no choice in the matter of who sits on the Supreme Court, and why are these people appointed for life? The last I heard, a person in a position for life was a "DICTATOR". These people were "NOT ELECTED BY THE PEOPLE". They were "APPOINTED "by people who wanted the country to be ruled by "People who thought like them". Just like a DICTATOR, who passes his *thoughts down to his sons, or Daughters, or family period, as long as the "authority to make decisions" stayed in the family. The Supreme Court "DICTATORS" gave us George Bush, and we SUFFERED for their mistake. "THE WHOLE WORLD SUFFERED FOR THEIR "MISTAKE", not just the United States. With the makeup of the Supreme Court, we're "DOOMED" to whatever "HORRIBLE DECISIONS" these people make. The "Citizens United" decision, "the HOBBY LOBBY DECISION" "The CIVIL RIGHTS DECISION", all of these were Devastating decisions that hurt MILLIONS of People, and yet we're "STUCK" with these people for LIFE? A lot of us will be under their tyrannical rule for the rest of our lives, because some of them are "YOUNGER THEN US". What makes it so bad, is the fact that their rulings in some cases makes it possible for them to live longer, and "we the people" to "DIE SOONER". Meanwhile we sit idly by while people* like Scalia, says and does outrageous things that offends millions of people, and we have no way of doing anything about it, and our politicians are too lazy to even attempt to do anything about it. Another bad JOKE ON THE AMERICAN PEOPLE IS, CLARENCE THOMAS. Here's a man who was "APPOINTED "by the first George Bush, under suspicion at the time, of being a sex offender, and yet, somehow he was confirmed. This man hasn't mumbled a word, or given an opinion on anything, in over 6 years. At least he knows his intelligence is suspect, and limited, I guess he's taking advice from a "Dirty Harry" movie where Clint Eastwood said, "A man's got to know his Limitations". Not only that, his big, Fat, sloppy wife is a big time "tea bagger", and works for tea party causes. They both attend tea bagger parties at expensive resorts, given by the Koch brothers, the Waltons, and other "BILLIONAIRES" and then he comes back and votes on tea bagger type related issues. Are we all a bunch of IDIOTS or what? Obviously we are, because he continues to say "go fuck yourself, I can do what I want to do" These are the very reasons that nobody should be "APOINTED TO THE SUPREME COURT FOR LIFE". You can't be "APPOINTED", or "ELECTED", to the Presidency for LIFE, so why the SUPREME COURT? What makes them so fucking special? Just think if RONALD RAY-GUN had been appointed to the Supreme Court for life. He would have "DIED" in that position "mumbling" to HIMSELF, and "DROOLING", like a fucking IDIOT. However, he still managed to "FUCK UP" the country before he became a babbling "IDIOT "and died. That's why the republicans have made him into so kind of Demented GOD. He proved to them that the Government couldn't do anything right, by not doing anything right, when he was in Government. He Fucked up the Government, did Illegal shit against the people of the United States, and the Government, Sold, or traded, illegal guns to our enemies, (IRAN), and the Contras, blatantly lied to the united States Congress, and then pointed his finger, and said "see all the ILLEGAL shit I did and got away with it" proves the U.S Government can't do anything right. "I should have been put in Jail by now". Now that's a man we should all admire. Those are the requirements to being a REAL REPUBLICAN, and not just a "RINO. He did all of this while he was on the way to Full blown DEMENTIA, or SENILITY. Yeah, the republicans sure know how to pick their HEROES, AND GODS don't they? I'm surprised they didn't pass legislation to change the laws so that he could run for 2 more terms.LOL After all, what are a few broken laws for such a GREAT man like RAY-GUN? Right today, we're still feeling the results of his trickle down economics, in the form of income inequality. You have to give him credit though, He was a rich mans, rich man. He really looked out for the 1%, and the rethugs who want to bring back the "good old days". In all *actuality though, the good old days are still with us. Wages are the same as they were then; there has been no advancement for the poor, and middleclass, thanks to the Bush administration who continued his policies. Labor unions,(RAY – GUNS favorite punching bag),have been depleted), poor people are poorer, the middleclass has dwindled down to almost nothing, the rich are paying almost no taxes, the poor are paying more taxes to make up for the rich not paying any. Those "BUCKS" that RAY-GUN saw at the grocery store buying Lobster, cigarettes, and expensive wine with food Stamps, are now starving like they should. Their wives, and kids, are starving too, that should make him roll over in his grave with glee. Minimum wage hasn't changed much. Yeah, a lot of things are still the same thanks to the republicans who LOVE, and ADMIRE RAY-GUN and his policies. We even have a BLACK, supposedly Democratic president, who I really suspect is a moderate republican, who loves RAY-*

GUN. He Quotes RAY-GUN all the time. He has nothing but praise for everything RAY-GUN DID. I'll bet you wonder why I call him RAY-GUN. Well the reason is because I think it was kind of Ironic the way he died. Everybody knows how unfeeling and hateful he was about poor people, Blacks, and their kids. He would do anything to make life miserable for the underprivileged. He even said at one time that poor kids shouldn't get vegetables with their free lunch because the Catsup was their vegetable because it was made out of tomatoes. The dummy didn't realize that tomatoes are a fruit. Back to my reason for calling him RAY-GUN. RAY-GUN, during his presidency at one point, didn't want poor people to get any type of free healthcare. That included mentally handicapped people, sick people, anybody who wasn't rich. That wasn't really anything new because everybody knows that's part of being a republican, you have to hate everybody, especially those not like you, or as fortune as you.

JAMES WITHERSPOON

Ray-gun started in on the social programs first. He had to figure out a way to take the little bit that poor people had, without looking like the piece of shit that he was. I guess he had a brainstorming meeting with the republicans, on how to steal, and take, from the poor without being too obvious. He came up with the bright idea of what I called "Zapping" all the funds for these social programs. The same way that the republicans like to defund things today. They claim they don't have the funds to keep these programs going so they give the money to the millionaires, and Billionaires, and OIL companies, etc, in the form of subsidies, and tax breaks. The way RAY-GUN did this without anybody noticing what he was doing was take the money away quietly? He would ZAP, this program a little, then ZAP, that Program a little, maybe a week later. For instance, you might be on food stamps this month, then next month you'll notice they were cut in half; Ray-Gun had ZAPPED YOU. Then the next month, you wouldn't receive anything, ZAP completed. Well, one day I was stuck in traffic in downtown Chicago. I was waiting for the light to change at Michigan, and Monroe, right in the middle of downtown. All of a sudden, I saw what looked like a man rising from the hood of my car. I knew I hadn't run over anybody but I didn't want to take any chances, so I got out of my car and walked to the front of the car, where the man was brushing himself off. I asked the man, "How did you get under my car? He said, "I wasn't under your car". I said, "Well where in the fuck did you come from? He pointed down and said "down there". I looked down where he was pointing, and there was a manhole with the cover open and pushed to the side. I asked him, "Did you come out of there?" He said "yeah" kind of indignantly, and walked off. Needless to say, I was puzzled, and wondering "what in the fuck was he doing down there? By now people behind me were honking their horns, and calling me all kinds of names, so I got back into my car, and drove away. A couple of hours later on my way back from traffic court, I was on the corner of Michigan Avenue and Roosevelt, when the car in front of me slammed on his brakes. I almost hit him in the ass and I was pissed because the light was green, and he shouldn't have hit his brakes. I leaned out of my window, and then I saw a man in front of the car in front of me. He was holding up his hands and shouting something about "STOP, don't you see the Kids? The guy in the car in front of me was laughing and trying to navigate around the guy in the street. I guess he'd always wanted to be a traffic cop. I finally got around the guy, and headed for the Southside. After arriving home, I mentioned something about the "Nuts "I had seen downtown. My "old lady" laughed and said didn't you hear about Ronald Reagan kicking all of the crazy people out of the "nut houses"? I didn't much care about politics back then, so I wasn't surprised that I hadn't heard about this. I came to find out that RAY-GUN had defunded all of the mental institutions, and there were "nuts" all over the streets with nowhere to go. Then I started paying attention to all of the "crazies "out there, and they were everywhere. I never much cared about who was president, or whether they were Democrats, or republicans, because neither one had much bearing on my life, nor where it was headed. My whole life was about schemes, and plots. You probably don't know what I'm talking about, and it would take me all day to explain it to you, so maybe I'll write another book, and tell you about it.LOL Anyway, I think that was the beginning of my paying more attention to politics, and the profound impact that they could make on your life. I never voted, even when Martin L King was making such a big fuss over it in the "60s ("Actually, I was too young to vote then anyway), and the civil rights act was passed in "64".I was aware of the civil rights issues, and I knew they would have something to do with my life one way or another because I was black. But I didn't really *care. I was making more money then anybody on a regular good paying job anyway, and I wasn't of legal age to even have a real job. Then, the murders started happening in Mississippi, and all over the South, and I began paying more attention. I began to wonder why White People hated the Idea of Black People voting so much. I soon found out that you had power in your vote. I also learned it wasn't just all white people; it was mostly the republicans who for whatever reasons hated the idea of black people voting, or doing anything progressive that would make their lives better. Besides, I had been warned by my family to never vote republican because they were hard core KKK members and such. I would hear my mother and her sisters arguing about how the republicans used to be the good guys, and the Democrats used to be the racists. At that time though the democrats were mostly in the south. It was all very confusing. Nowadays, the script has totally flipped. The republicans are the NEW JIM CROW, and the*

Tea baggers are the new KKK. Funny, how times change, but still stay the same. The roles are the same, the player's just change. I've also learned that most of the good things that have happened to this country has been accomplished by Democrats, and fought against tooth and nail, by the Republicans. It didn't really take me long to figure that one out though. Social Security, unemployment insurance ,Medicare Medicaid, food stamps, healthcare, civil rights, women's rights, gay rights, minimum wage increases, although they lag behind where they should be, veterans benefits, you name it, everything and anything that benefits poor, and working people in general was accomplished by the "Dems". Each and every one of the things I just named has been fought against by the republicans, and they don't try to hide it. They're the party of the rich, the super rich, the millionaires, the billionaires, the insurance companies, the Oil companies, big pharmaceutical companies, and the Super stupid

.anything that the costs you a lot of money. Their job is to help these companies keep gouging you; and robbing you blind. They have marching orders as lobbyists, and lawmakers to keep the big companies rolling in money, while the poor people are struggling to buy their services. They dutifully make laws in the dark of night when nobody is looking, that makes it easy for big corporations to operate at 500 or 600 % profit margins, while helping them through tax cuts funnel away Billions upon Billions of dollars. As we all know, there are a whole lot less Millionaires and Billionaires in this country then there are regular hard working people. These corporations, and rich people could not, and would not exist without the help of a whole lot of uneducated, racist, ignorant mean, hateful people, who through lack of common sense and intelligence, vote against themselves. It's no coincidence that most of your red states are also your most poverty ridden states. They have the worst schools, the highest unemployment, and the most are "right to work states". We all know,(at least those of us who don't live there),that "right to work "means "right to work for nothing". For some reason, the people in these states don't understand that. They will defend and vote for the very people who put them in that position. So much for the GOP talking points that the American people are "SMART". That's a lie whether a Democrat says it or a republican says it. I know it's not smart politics to call people "stupid,", but when you continually kick yourself in the ass, somebody needs to quit lying to you, and maybe help you see what you're doing wrong. Would you lie to your kid and tell him he's the smartest kid in school, when you know he's one of the dumbest? Of course not. You would try to show him how to improve his chances of learning. The republicans seem to get away with saying "It's smart of you to vote for me you dummy, and I'm not going to do a god damn thing for you". Reason #5.Impeach Obama for playing to the republican base at the expense of the lives of thousands of young black kids rotting away in jail, for smoking a joint. It's really shameful and disgusting when Obama sits around mute, while Rand Paul comes to the defense of these kids. RAND PAUL, a known racist, trying to put on like he's a libertarian. However, Paul has some good talking points, and knows how to deliver them. He also knows Obama is afraid to talk about helping black kids and black people in general. Paul takes advantage of Obama's fear of Republicans, by saying things he knows other republicans, or Obama can't say. He doesn't seem to care about what Dems, or Rethugs think. He seems to be in his own little world. He knows however, that he has to change stories in mid stream, if he gets within striking distance of the presidency. Of course Rand Paul has no problem denying saying anything. He will tell you in a New York minute that he didn't say something, even though you have him on television, and in the news saying it.

JAMES WITHERSPOON

In other words he's a *BALD FACED LIAR*. He plagiarizes other peoples work, and denies it, even though you have the proof right in front of you. It's kind of funny if you look at it. So anyway, he steps in and brings up the conversation, under the guise that it's too expensive to keep incarcerating these black kids for nothing. It even sounds good to me, but I know I could never vote for him. He doesn't really believe that anyway, he just likes to rub it in Obama's face that he cares more about black kids then Obama does, and maybe he has a point. reason #6. Impeach Obama for sitting around idly by while a whole city in the United States is going without drinking water, water to bath in, or take a shower, and even water to flush your toilet. Yeah, that's right. I'm talking about a major big city in this country. Detroit. Of course we all know that Obama can't even mention this city because it has such a large Black population. I'm not sure what Obama can do to help Detroit, but the last time I checked, Detroit was a part of the United States. The republicans want Obama to help White people who live   clean on the other side of the world, but you haven't heard them say a word about helping those poor people with out water in Detroit. It's as if they don't exist in OBAMALAND. The reasons I gave you that the republicans could use to Impeach OBAMA, would never be used, because all of them are against republican philosophy. Number 1 and 2, would never work because let's face it, Obama would never do anything to hurt BUSH, and Cheney. #3,4, and 5 would be next to impossible because they would have to help black people in order to use them. Their policies are the reason that all of those young Black kids are in Jail in the first place. As for the Black man that the Staten Island police MURDERED the other day, I'm still waiting on Eric Holder's Injustice dept to at least threaten to prosecute somebody. After all, this murder by the police was captured on somebody's cell phone camera, or something. Anyway, it ended up on TV, and is seen by the whole world. I'll bet you there are people in England, and France wondering why they haven't heard any mention of this by Obama. Well guess what, if you think Obama is going to weigh in on a BLACK MAN being MURDERED by the Police dept, you have to think again. It aint gonna happen. Just for the hell of it, I'm going to see how long it takes before Obama even Mentions this. If this had been a white man being choked to death in public, he would have had a press conference the next day. To all of you black folks out there, I apologize if you think that I'm being too hard on Obama, but you need to open up your eyes, and face the truth. After all, you're living in a time of the first, and probably the last, Black president of the United States. You're living History, you might as well understand what you're looking at. Obama really does have some things that he could probably be Impeached for, but not the nonsense that the republicans want to impeach him for. The republicans say Obama is Lawless. That's like saying "Urkel is a Gangster". Who's lawless is the fuck ups on Wall Street that OBAMA, and Holder, still refuse to prosecute. IMPEACH him for not sending your republican Wall Street buddies to jail, if you really want to impeach him. IMPEACH him for letting those innocent men in Guantanamo bay rot in jail without a trial. IMPEACH him for letting the banks get away with theft, fraud, and all of their other white collar crimes. IMPEACH him for ignoring BLACK PEOPLE being MURDERED on the streets by policemen for selling a cigarette. IMPEACH OBAMA for ignoring those Black kids rotting away in jail for nothing. NO, you wouldn't ever think about IMPEACHING him for any of those reasons because you approve of all of those HORRIBLE things. Those are things that you're responsible for, and he's doing a good job pacifying you and your republican GANG. In a perfect world, the whole entire republican Congress should be arrested under the RICO ACT. You've heard of that I'm sure. It's Racketeer Influenced and Corrupt Organization ACT. That definition fits the republican Congress to a "T". Yes sir, in a perfect world you would "ALL" be behind bars for high Treason, as traitors to your country. This republican Congress would rather DESTROY this country, then to see a Black man improve anything in it. Especially, improve anything for the Black people in this country. You don't have to worry. Obama hasn't improved ANYTHING for Black people in his 2 terms in office yet, and as a lame duck president, I don't see him improving anything before he leaves office. A lot of people call you the "DO NOTHING CONGRESS". I don't think that's true. I think Congress did what they set out to do, that was "keep OBAMA FROM DOING ANYTHING". They systematically "FROZE" this country in time for the last 5, going on 6 years. While the rest of the world has moved on they've built trains that go 300 miles an hour, made great progress in HYBRID cars, improved the economy in some of their countries, and accepted the jobs that our greedy politicians helped send them. Meanwhile, our infrastructure is rotting away, and collapsing, and our politicians are making laws that make it easier for us to kill each other. The Billionaires in this country have bought our politicians, our Supreme Court, and our news Media. Oh yes, we don't want to forget our news media. They have been complicit in everything that has been going on wrong in this country. The Republican Party is led by a FAT, DRUG ADDICTED, SLOB, who hates everybody, from women and kids, to BLACKS, and OTHER WHITES that don't agree with him. When you follow a piece of shit like him, it doesn't say very much for you. You have to be a "DUMB MOTHERFUCKER", be led around by the ring in your stupid ass nose, by a drug addled Idiot, spewing a lot of unnecessary HATE. Wait a minute, maybe I spoke too soon. After all, this man is FILTHTY RICH, I guess HATE is profitable. Maybe if I could find a bunch of IDIOTS to listen to a bunch of bullshit, and HATE, maybe I could make me 30 or 40 million a year too. After all, the Government even let's the American Military listen to him spewing his HATE speeches all over the airwaves from what I've heard. Maybe he and I could have a show together. He could tell me about how happy the slaves were to have 3 hots and a cot, and I could tell him how much I would like to stick my dick in his hateful mouth, to make him shut up. Obviously, I've strayed off the conversation that I was supposed to be on. Anyway, back to the people who call themselves patriots, but hate the United States Government, I have one thing to say to you. You're "full of SHIT". That's right. "FULL OF SHIT".I don't know if you might have noticed, but 99% of the people on TV, or cable, or however you happen to get your news, that say they hate the Government are "WHITE". That's right, the people that the

United States Government have done the most for, hate "US". The reason I say US" is because "WE THE PEOPLE" are the GOVERNMENT.I don't know how many of you have ever heard of Joan Walsh, but she's a contributor on MSNBC news, and also I think, a hell of an Author. She's also an editor at Salon.com, and blogger, whatever that is. Anyway, she wrote a book about how white people miss the good old days that never were. I thought a lot of it was kind of funny because the things that she said in her book were exactly what I've always thought about white people who "hate" the Government. What a lot of illiterate people don't understand is that the "Gummermint" that they hate so bad, built the middleclass in this country after World War 2, or WWII.They didn't build a "BLACK MIDDLECLASS", they built a "WHITE MIDDLECLASS". One of the reasons they didn't want Blacks in the military was because they knew the benefits that they were going to bestow on the returning soldiers, and they didn't want to be giving them to a lot of "NEGROES", or "NIGGERS", as they liked to call them. You see, your most hardcore racists are "OLD WHITE PEOPLE" who remember when they were given preferential treatment over Blacks and other minorities. Other then Indians, most of the people in this country were Immigrants, and still are. Blacks ancestors have been here longer then most of these white people's ancestors. Yet, Blacks have always been discriminated against worst then any other people in this country. The reason that some white people hate the Government so much now is because the Government isn't as racist as it once was. You see, Blacks have always paid their taxes just like everybody else in this country, so when you gave all of those white Veterans houses, and all the other VA benefits, you were basically giving them Black peoples money also. When they gave all of the white people the good jobs, and left the black people out, of jobs, it wasn't because black people were "lazy", it was because they wouldn't let them work. All of the welfare, social Security, Medicare, VA benefits, jobs, credit, Help ,and any kind of assistance was sucked up by the "WHITE PEOPLE ".Because of this racist bullshit, right today, a white man on Social Security, will get a much bigger check then a black man on Social Security. The reason for that is because the system is still rigged against the Black Man. The white man made more when he was working, so he gets more when he retires. SIMPLE. The Old ass veterans from WWII are some of your most vicious racists. The sooner they all die off the better. They were used to being the recipients of all the "gummermint" had to give, and they didn't want the "gummermint" to give anybody else anything. They in turn taught their kids to "HATE" the people who they thought the Government was helping besides them. In other words, "You could be giving me more, if you weren't helping those lazy ass Niggers too". Those same niggers that you think of as the "other people "have been getting the short end of the stick all of their lives, and they continue to get the short end of the stick. What you have is a system of Racism that the politicians keep going through the laws they make. That's why I think so little of Obama's presidency. As far as Black people are concerned there's little HOPE, and there has been no CHANGE. It's no accident that they came up with a way to make criminals out of Black kids, for "crack" cocaine, and at the same time give white kids a slap on the wrist for powdered cocaine. This country was "BUILT" on "RACISM", and will one day "IMPLODE" because of "RACISM". The really smart white people in this country know that we can't continue on this path of inequality, and are trying to do something about it, while the ingrained racists think it can go on indefinitely. However, a strange thing has happened recently. Well maybe not recently, but it started about 33 years ago in 1981 when Ronald RAY GUN was elected President.

Ray GUN set into motion a downward spiral that would affect the middleclass like never before. While he preached one thing, he did another. He harped on "not raising taxes", but what he meant was "no taxes for the rich". He raised taxes over, and over, again, but mostly on the little people. He also went about destroying the unions. That made it easier for the big corporations to hire people at lower wages because they had no say so about their wages anymore, or should I say no representation. The big corporations also didn't have to worry about strikes. The unions have always been the backbone of the "white" middle class. I say the "white" middleclass because "Blacks weren't allowed", in those unions. The unions kept black men out of the unions by only hiring people in their families. When they needed help at a union job, it was common practice to tell someone on the job to bring in somebody in their family. If you brought in a friend, he'd better be white. At that time there wasn't much race mixing, so there was little chance of some white guy bringing in a black friend. These days, you see a lot of blacks and whites who are real friends. I actually have white friends myself. Anyway, Reagan was a liar, underhanded, and actually performed a lot of criminal acts while he was in office as president. He put Nixon to shame. Nixon was a choir boy compared to him. Nixon got thrown out of office for a cover-up, Reagan got "CAUGHT", lying to Congress, trading weapons to our enemies,(IRAN),and some other shit about the contras. He was a one man crime spree. That's why the republicans love him so much. He's something like a Jesse James hero to them. I guess they look at him as some kind of romantic criminal hero because he lied to the American People and his country about his illegal activities, and got away with it. Ronald RAY GUN should have been our first American President to go to jail, at least for a couple of years. However, a lot of people think that today's republicans wouldn't accept him because he wasn't as good a liar as they are today.

JAMES WITHERSPOON

I guess his racism, and dogging the poor wasn't enough for them today. I think he would fit in just fine. All he would have to do is go on fox follies, and let them tell him what to say to be as big an IDIOT as the rest of them are. At least he had an excuse for doing some of the dirt he did, he could always say he was having a senior moment, and didn't realize what the fuck he was doing. As I was saying earlier in the book, Karma got a hold of his ass. After throwing all of those poor, mentally ill people out into the street with his bullshit policies, he ended up just as fucked up as they were. He was just in a better house, and had more money I guess. It's still Karma though. He ended up leeching off the Government he despised, and hated so much. All republicans hate the Government unless it's doing something for them. I don't understand why you don't have to take a pledge saying you won't try to destroy the very Government that you work for. These people do absolutely nothing for the money we pay them except Obstruct, and shut down our Government. They should at least be fired, and made to reimburse the American people for their lack of doing ANYTHING. Every one of those son of a bitches that don't want the American people to have healthcare, should NOT be allowed to have healthcare, at our expense.. Yet, they have no qualms, nor do they have any shame about accepting their free healthcare, while we have to die if we don't have any money to purchase healthcare .Anyway, since Reagan brought on these draconian policies, this country has gone downhill. Income inequality is at an all time high, poverty has sky rocketed, and unions are at an all time low. We now have a supreme court that is stacked against the people, and from the looks of it, it's going to get worse. The Supreme Court is a republican Joke on the American people. They think that corporations are people. No, I'm not going to fall for that. They know that corporations aren't people, but they can't come out and say that they've been bought, and paid for by the billionaires, and corporations. Yeah, while we weren't looking, the middleclass has shrunk. I predict that if we don't do something about this soon, like within the next 10 years, we won't have a Democracy. We don't really have one now. What we have, is a few Billionaires who have bought our lives through our politicians. They have undermined our whole political system right before our very eyes, and there's nothing we can do about it. The republicans have lied, and cheated by making our vote useless through gerrymandering our elections so that no matter what we do, we can't hardly vote them out or kick them out. By the way, today there was a news flash that said that Obamacare is in danger of losing coverage for over 5 million people because of some kind of wording error in the paperwork. The republicans are jumping with Glee. I'll never understand how stopping other people from getting medical attention, can make another person Happy. It really makes no sense. They want to actually see children, and poor people die. It's unbelievable that in this day and age, there are EVIL people like that. These people belong in the Stone Age, where it's every man for himself. They don't belong in a civil society. When you're that heartless, and mean spirited, you should just go off somewhere and blow your fucking brains out. Who would give a fuck? Well, this is a book that started out as a helpful guide to help the rethugs Impeach Obama, but I got a little carried away. That happens sometime when you're having fun. I guess you figured out by now that a lot of this has been said tongue in cheek, and I don't really want to "IMPEACH OBAMA". I would never do anything to help the Rethugs do anything against Obama. However, I do think he needs to MAN UP, and quit kissing their asses . It gets sickening. Another "little shout out "to Obama, They've never liked you, and they're never going to like you, get over it. As a matter of fact, they HATE YOU, *with a passion. I guess this is like a short letter to Obama: Obama, you won both elections. You succeeded in catching, and killing Osama Bin Laden, you got Obamacare passed, something that will save countless lives, and make millions of people's lives a lot easier. Contrary to what the Republicans say, or do, at this point, there's nothing they can do to tarnish that. Even if they succeed in killing it, it will make them look like the Assholes that they are. You also finally got us out of Iraq, and on the way out of Afghanistan. You have a lot of accomplishments that can never be taken away from you. You saved the auto industry, in spite of all the negative bullshit, and obstructionism from the Republicans, and Fox Follies. These people will forever hate you with a passion for these very same accomplishments. They are not in any way going to let up on you in the next 2 ½ years left in your Presidency. That, you can count on, or take to the bank, as they say. With all the hate aimed your way by these maniacs* or so called Congressmen, I have been worried to death about you Brother. I look at the way John Boehner stares at the back of your head when you are on stage together, and to me there's PURE HATE there. I know, and you know, he's a drunk, but I wouldn't take a chance with him standing behind me. I believe with all of my heart that they wish someone would assassinate you. With all of the people like stupid ass Sarah Palin around threatening people with guns, you need to be extra vigilant. Don't trust these people, and stay the hell out of Texas, Arizona, and Mississippi for that matter. These states are full of hateful people. That's not the only thing I want to tell you. As much abuse as you have taken from your enemies, I guess you should be able to take a little constructive criticism from a friend. You need to release those black kids in prison for smoking a joint, before it's too late for them. It is well documented that you, and just about every other president before you, got high off something, especially George Bush. He was a known cocaine, and alcohol abuser. Yet, you sit there in the highest office in the land, and twittle your thumbs while they rot in jail. Yet, Bush, and Cheney, walk around everyday, free as a bird, and they're both Mass murderers. Jail can make a person PRETTY DAMN MEAN, especially when you haven't done anything. I know this from experience. This Marijuana BULLSHIT has ruined many black kids LIVES. The white cops on the street won't take a white kid to jail for this nonsense because they know it can ruin them for life. These same white cops would lock up my child or yours at the drop of a hat, for the same reason, BECAUSE THEY KNOW IT WILL RUIN THAT BLACK KIDS LIFE. This is what we're dealing with here. You need DO SOMETHING for your own people before you leave office. All you ever, talk about is IMMIGRATION. At what point do you stand up for BLACK PEOPLE? Do we all have to turn Hispanic for you to decide to help us? We

DON'T need fatherhood lectures, we need
DECENT paying jobs. We don't need a black
President afraid to say the word POOR. Most of
us are not so called: MIDDLECLASS. I'm sure
you've noticed that, and that's the reason you only
talk about the MIDDLECLASS. I can hear your
advisors now telling you to stay away from the
word POOR, because it's bad for your image.
Yeah, the image of you being concerned about
black people. We wouldn't want anybody to think
you care about black people would we? If I sound
angry it's because I AM. This has been going on
for your entire time in office. You knew a long
time ago that while the Feds were still raiding
Marijuana dispensaries in states that had legalized
medicinal Marijuana those more, and more, black
kids were going to end up in prison. You knew
that the owners of these stores weren't going to
jail, because they would more than likely be white,
but the regular kids on the streets would for sure,
and more then likely, they would be Black. That's

JAMES WITHERSPOON

all the police wanted, enough young black kids to fill up their jails and prisons. I hope like hell, you can come up with some kind of plan to have this SHIT taken off their records, otherwise, these kids will be marked FOR LIFE. After all is aid and done, when you leave office, I don't really see a whole lot to point to, that I can say you did for black people, and THAT'S sad. It shows that the Republicans succeeded after all. Their main objective was to keep you so distracted, that you wouldn't have time to help your own people. You can help Mexicans, or any other brown people, but you'd better not try to help them NIGGERS. By the way, where's your indignation about the MURDER of this black man who the cops choked to death, on TV the other day over allegedly selling a loose cigarette? See, these are the kind of things I'm talking about. Why haven't you said anything? You immediately said something about somebody in Benghazi getting killed, and he was in a war zone, thousands of miles away from here, but you're mute about a black man being murdered right here in the United States on Staten Island, in broad daylight, in front of countless witnesses, by a pack of murderous white cops. What are you going to do? Have a beer with the cop who choked him to death, and killed him? And where is Eric Holder, and his Injustice Dept? Is he going to investigate this, or are you going to tell him to turn a blind eye again, like he does constantly for the criminals on Wall Street? You expect this kind of shit from a Republican President like George Bush , but you don't expect this shit from a Black Democratic President. As sad as it might be Obama, your presidency is NOT going to go down in history as a time of great prosperity, or even a little bit of advancement in the lives of black people. The Republicans seceded in achieving their main goal, which was the continued oppression of the Black race in the United States. This could only have been achieved with your help, by that I don't mean that you consciously did anything against Black people in this country, I mean that you did more harm than good to the image of the American Black Man than any white man could have ever done. The way you did that was by showing this constant, never ending foot dragging, and meek, fearful, image of the Black Man. I'm sure there is some White Author out there who is going to one day tell the truth about your 2 terms in office, and about your lack of interest in any advancement of your OWN People. Don't think for a minute that I think that you could have shown any bravery without a lot of backlash from white people, but you could of at least made an effort. That's the end of my personal letter to you. I hope anyone reading this doesn't think I'm being to hard on you.

Anyway, as I wind this down, there's one more subject I would like to dwell on for a moment. That subject is so controversial that I'm almost afraid to bring it up, and I'm not known for being "bashful". One of the reasons

JAMES WITHERSPOON

I wrote the "letter to Obama" was to give you an insight into how your image can in effect, control how people react to other people. Growing up in Chicago, I learned a long time ago, that your image or reputation could be the difference between "life and Death". Chicago is, and will always be a rough, tough, and deadly place, even more so now, then ever before. How you carry yourself makes all the difference in the world, on whether you survive it or not. This isn't an over exaggeration. This is a fact. You learn that when you say something, you have to mean it. The people AROUND" you, as well as the people who know "OF YOU," must know that you don't take "NO SHIT", NO TIME","NO WHERE". Those are the "3 NOs" of most large, urban cities, not just Chicago. Your very life can depend on that philosophy. From my experience growing up under these conditions, I knew that the more

"DANGEROUS" you were, the fewer problems you would have. If you were the type of person who forgave everything somebody said, or did, to you, or against you, you were in for a rough, miserable life. You were going to have to fight, cut shoot, stab, bite, kick, and anything, and everything else you could, to survive. If you didn't take "NO SHIT" from the beginning, you wouldn't have those problems. You see, "BULLIES" have a "feeling" or a sort of "RADAR", for weakness, and they act on it. When a Bully comes upon a group of people, they automatically search for the "weakest "amongst them. Once you're "marked "as the "weak one" they go to work. You'll never have any peace in your life, if you're the one they "mark". That's why I say the republicans remind me of a "Gang". They look for weakness, and they pounce, like the predators they are. They saw this "go along," to "get along," attitude in Obama, and they pounced. This isn't confined to Obama; it's their "Ideology". They prey on Women, Children, Gays, Lesbians, seniors, minorities, poor people, anybody they think is vulnerable, and has "no power". Some people see these "bullies" as "strong", and follow them. They think that as long as the bully has someone else to pick on, they won't notice "THEM". These people are "COWARDS", and "bullies in training". These people are the "bully's Base", or Gang. They're weaker then the people they help the bully push around, but they don't see it that way. They're the bully's cowardly SHEEP. They go along with whatever the bully does, out of fear that they're next. They don't have enough courage to say "this is wrong", and I don't want any part of this". Over a period of time, these "bullies in training", lose all RESPECT for the people they think are "weak", and in reality, they lose all RESPECT, for themselves. They don't think of themselves as "BULLIES", they think of themselves as the "STRONG" ones", and their victims as the "WEAK" ones,"or the "PUSSIES".I say all of this to say, that in my eyes, I see Obama as part of the problem he has been having with the rethuglican party all of this time. In other words he showed them "weakness from the beginning". Once he turned his "MANHOOD "over to them, it was "ALL OVER" but the "boo hoo ing". (That means crying) in the streets. Yes, I'm accusing Obama of creating his own problems with the "republican Bullies "Himself. If he had stopped their "Bullshit" from the beginning, I really believe his presidency would end on a more positive note .Most of his wounds were self inflicted. From the first time that that ignorant piece of shit Joe Wilson hollered out "YOU LIE", he should have taken action. Obama has a fast, sharp mind, and a sharp tongue. As president of the United States, I'm sure he could have simply said "REMOVE THAT MAN". That embarrassment would have made everybody else think twice about pulling a stunt like that again. At the least Obama should have said something like, "ignorance like that is why we can't get anything done", and get along with each other. That would have infuriated the republican bullies, and maybe they would have all gotten up and walked out. That would have proved just how ignorant they ALL were. INSTEAD, he stood there and looked embarrassed as if he had said something wrong. What Joe Wilson did was set the stage for many more embarrassing moments for this president. He set the stage for the "Birther bullshit, and lots of other lies about Obama. You see, one thing you can NEVER do with a BULLY is ignore him. Bullies take SILENCE as "WEAKNESS".

JAMES WITHERSPOON

Obama gave them the Go ahead to do what the fuck they wanted to do by never responding to their attacks. I'm sure Obama heard about how President Clinton stopped their lies and nonsense when he was President. Clinton started what he called a RAPID RESPONSE ROOM. Their job was to answer any LIES, and made up bullshit, within 24 hours of the time it was told. It worked just great. However, they still didn't treat Clinton with nearly as much disrespect as they have this man .Also, the REASON behind their "HATRED" of this man is the mitigating factor. They hate him because "OF HIS RACE", and nothing more. They don't really think he's lawless, that's nonsense, they don't think he's disobeying the constitution, he's a law professor, they know better. They hate him simply because he's black, and nothing else. I could go on, and on, about why they hate him but I'm sure anybody reading this knows why, without me telling them, and they know it's true. The fact that Obama is president must be hard to explain when you've been telling your kids how "SUPERIOR" whites are to blacks, all this time, and then there's OBAMA on TV making a lie out of you. That can be kind of embarrassing. Therefore, you have to bring him down as much as you possibly can with lies. The truth hurts. I'm going to ease into this other topic nice and slow, so that you can get a full understanding of what I'm about to say. Today, I happen to be looking at the JON STEWART show, or "THE DAILY SHOW", and his guest was the Gay guy, George Takei, of Star Wars Fame. Jon Stewart asked Mr. Takei about the internment of the Japanese during WWII. Mr. Takei told Stewart about how the American soldiers came to his home with guns drawn, and ordered his family out and took all of them to an internment camp surrounded by barbed wire in Arkansas. Other Japanese families were taken to places like the Nevada desert, the Arizona Desert, UTAH, AND Colorado or somewhere else, equally as miserable. He said he remembered how they had to pledge allegiance to the American flag everyday before they started school,(yes they had school), and how ironic he thought that was that they were treated like criminals just because they looked like the people(the Japanese),that bombed Pearl Harbor on December 7th 1941. It was kind of touching. However, he never said that they were mistreated or tortured or anything that came close to that. They were fed well, and were there only until the war ended in 1945.The United States didn't enter the war until 1941, when the Japanese bombed Pearl Harbor. On February 19th, 1942, President Roosevelt issued executive order 9066 authorizing the interment of the Japanese *families. It mostly depended on where they lived geographically, so they were there about 3 ½ or 4 years. Years later, in 1980 under pressure from the Japanese American Citizens League, then president Jimmy Carter, ordered an investigation into whether the Government was justified in putting these people in internment camps. He appointed the (CWRIC), or "Commission on wartime relocation and internment of civilians". In 1988, under Ronald Reagan, the "CIVIL LIBERTIES ACT" was signed into law, which apologized for their internment on behalf of the United States Government, and authorized the payment of $20,000 to each individual camp survivor. The Government admitted that the internment was based on RACIAL PREJUDICE, hysteria, and a failure of political leadership. The U.S Government eventually disbursed more then $1.6Billion in "REPARATIONS "to 82,219*

Japanese Americans, and their Heirs, who had been interned. Now, I guess you can see where I'm going with this. Now, these people were "NOT ENSLAVED". They were "NOT TORTURED, "they were NOT "HUNG". They didn't work sun up, and sun down, until they "DIED"."They DID NOT BUILD THIS COUNTRY WITH FREE LABOR".BLACK PEOPLE, or their Ancestors,(MY PEOPLE) DID NOT ATTACK THIS COUNTRY, in any way ,shape, fashion, OR FORM. I find it hard to believe that Ronald Reagan had that much compassion, and was willing to give that kind of money to any kind of minority though. There HAD to be some kind of political catch to him doing anything for anybody who wasn't rich, or white. The only thing I can think of is: Maybe he figured that this was a good way that he could buy the Asian vote, or maybe he could trick the Asians into being Republicans for a generation, I don't know, After all, He gave Amnesty to over 3 million Mexicans for political reasons. So, what would he care about giving away $1.6 Billion of the Governments money, to the Japanese? That way he could say the Government couldn't do anything right, while he was busy fucking the Government up. I think that was a smart move. Now today's republicans have gone and fucked that up. This country has no problem giving out "REPARATIONS" to anyone as long as they're not Black. Yet no one has ever been treated worse then the black man in this country. When they interned the Japanese, they didn't separate husbands and wives from their children. They didn't SELL them Like "CATTLE". They were only interned for a couple of years, and they got $20.000 a piece for that. Yet blacks were enslaved from Birth to death for hundreds of years. In a way, I can understand where the white man is coming from, because if the BLACK man was paid what he is really owed, "THIS COUNTRY WOULD BE BROKE". Yet, here we have a BLACK PRESIDENT, who has been trained by the white man to not even consider looking into REPARATIONS for the black people of this country. As a matter of fact Obama won't even say "POOR". I'll bet you a donut to a dollar, that if OBAMA ever said the word "poor" and "BLACK" in the same sentence he would throw up. I wonder what gave Jimmy Carter the courage to do what he did for the Japanese. That took a lot of courage. That's probably why the Republicans still hate him right today. I'll bet they worry that One of these days, a Democrat president is going to have the "Guts" to look into Reparations for BLACKS. I know I'll never see that day, but maybe, just maybe, my great, Great, grandchildren will be so lucky. However, at the rate we are going now, that might take another 100 years to bear fruit. I recently read where a white republican Politician from Mississippi, or one of those other southern states said "if I ever have to pay reparations to Blacks in this country, I'll stop paying Taxes". That just goes to show you the mindset of a lot of white, racist, bigoted, assholes in this country. You can believe he speaks for a lot of people in America. In the meantime, trying to IMPEACH OBAMA for all of the wrong reasons, rings hollow, and only helps divide this country more then it already is. It also weakens the Republican Party, because sooner or later, the nitwits who vote republican are going to wake up and smell the coffee. Obama will have come and gone, and I doubt if we'll have really learned anything from this period in our history. I don't really believe there's a cure for racism, but if you look around, you see more and more race interaction. You see more and more interracial marriages, of ALL races, not just Black and white. You see all kinds of people hanging out together. More people living anywhere they can afford to live and more tolerance of people not like other people. In the end, I believe it will do just like OLD PEOPLE, just "dry up and die". IN THE MEANTIME, "IMPEACH OBAMA". Well it's getting close to the mid term elections, and all of a sudden these Idiots are talking about all this IMPEACH SHIT again. They don't really want to Impeach Obama. They know what happened when they did that to Clinton. Plus, Obama has been using reverse psychology on them. He keeps saying shit about them impeaching him and suing him, (dumb ass Boehner's idea), and the Democrats have been raising money like crazy. The more the republicans talk about "impeachment", the more money they Democrats raise. One thing about Obama, he seems to always figure out a way to get his way. He pisses off his base, and then he comes back and does something really smart. I think that's what makes the rethugs so angry. They get so mad at him that they say, and do dumb shit, that makes themselves look "petty, and stupid". It's almost like they can't help themselves. On the same token, this republican Congress has an approval rating of about 7%, so they can't look much worse then they already do. I guess they figure they don't have much to lose, so what the fuck. Anyway, it's almost August, and the republicans are all psyched up to go on another long ass recess, and waste more of the taxpayer's money. What the fuck are they taking a recess from? They haven't done anything since Obama has been in office. These are the same Motherfuckers who keep talking about other people being lazy? These are the same people that think other people don't deserve to make more then minimum wage? See, that's the very reason that people HATE POLITICIANS so much. They have this entitlement complex like they're worth every penny they make, and they're being paid for doing absolutely "nothing". These are the same "pieces of shit" that do everything in their power to make life miserable for Poor, working people? It's amazing to say the least. There's one more subject that I want to touch on, before I end this book. That's the subject of Hillary Clinton. I really like Hillary but I don't really think she is going to make a good President. Everybody knows she has a lot of corporate, and wall street ties, and Ideas. She thinks we have to keep kissing the bigwigs asses to get along with them. I have this strange feeling that she has already had meetings with them that we don't even know about. I also think she has sold out to them before she even gets into office. I just wish

JAMES WITHERSPOON

like hell that Elizabeth Warren would change her mind, and run against Hillary. Elizabeth Warren is one of a kind, and I hate it that we will probably have to wait until Hillary serves 8 years before she throws her hat in the ring. I think Warren would run if she didn't like Hillary so much. Either one of them would win anyway. The thing that really gets me excited about Warren is that Wall Street is terrified of her. She's their worst Nightmare, and they know it. I'll bet they're hoping and praying that she comes nowhere near the White House, other then to visit Hillary. Also, I notice how quiet the wall Street Journal is about Warren running. The republicans are quiet as church mice about warren. They know their lobbying days would be over if she was to ever get in office. You see, Elizabeth Warren has a habit of doing what she says, unlike most politicians. She's honest, and cares about other people. She's

JAMES WITHERSPOON

also not an empty skirt. She's highly intelligent, and the kind of person who can make everybody join together, and get things done. She's really a White, FEMALE, version of BARACK OBAMA. Obama has a lot of accomplishments since he has been president, in spite of all the obstructionism he has had put in front of him. He also could have been a real, healing force between the races, if the republicans, and fox follies hadn't been stroking the fires of "HATE" everyday since he has been in office. There's no telling what Obama could have done if this country wasn't consumed with "HATRED" the way it is. Every republican politician in Congress has used Hate to get into their jobs, since Obama's been president. Their litmus test has been, "you've got to be a racist, and you must "Hate OBAMA", NOT the democratic party, but OBAMA PERSONALLY. Anybody who even "TOUCHED OBAMA" physically had to go.

JAMES WITHERSPOON

I guess nothing has changed much in America, and it just took a BLACK MAN getting elected President, to bring out all of the hidden racial Hatred still in this country. Obama has served this country admirably in spite of all the lies and ignorance of his opponents. He has persevered in spite of all of the made up scandals that they've thrown at him. He has managed to somehow look the other way when they call him names that no other president has ever been called. He's a much more tolerant person then I am, and then I could ever be. I've always believed in an eye for an eye, and a tooth for a tooth, but that doesn't make it right just because I believe that. I think that for some reason, I've felt all along that when they insulted Obama, they insulted me. I believe that a lot of black people feel that same way. Therefore it makes it easier for Obama to dismiss Black people because he knows that we will back him no matter what. He doesn't have to do anything to get our vote. He also knows that to keep the Hispanic vote, he has to "KEEP PRODUCING". The truth of the matter is, when the smoke settles, the Hispanics will exceed way beyond where the blacks have progressed too. Blacks will be right back where they started from, behind the eight ball. The most discouraging thing about all of this, is that we have a BLACK MAN in power who is so intimidated by the white establishment,(republicans),that he is willing to sacrifice his own peoples love ,admiration, and respect for him, to satisfy his enemies whims. The fact is, Obama doesn't have the same loyalty to black people as they have for him. There is no explanation as to why Obama cares more about Hispanic issues then he does BLACK issues. If we had a Hispanic president right today, he wouldn't give a fuck about anything concerning Black people. He *would be concerned about what's going on with the Hispanic population in America. Black people would be an after thought. Marco Rubio, knows or should know, that he will never be president, because he knows that as much as he Hates Obama, Republicans will never put a motherfuckering Hispanic in office. They still look at him as a MEXICAN, even though he's a Cuban. The poor ass republicans don't know the difference between a Mexican, and a Cuban, or any other nationality that speaks Spanish. As far as they are concerned, if you speak Spanish, you're a Mexican. They will always look at him as the "other". They think that he would open up the "FLOOD GATES TO HELL". It has always tickled me to death, when Rubio, and Herman Cain, were running for President that they actually thought that it was a possibility. The fact is that they knew better, they were only in it for the hell of it, and the* money. They know now, as they knew then, that they were only being "used" by the republicans. There's no way in holy hell that Herman Cain was going to ever be nominated by the republicans to be president. They even had him leading the other candidates for a short while. That was hilarious to me. Think about it. You would have a BLACK MAN running against another Black man, so whatever happens, you would have a black man for president. It was a "joke" to me, but I often wondered if I was the only person in America who saw it this way. I never heard any news pundits, or politicians talk about, or mention this, Democrat or Republican. It was as if this was a possibility. That's totally brain dead, and the republicans knew it. By the same token, there was no way that Rubio was going too far either. There was no way that He was going to let the "HORDES" of Mexicans, or Hispanics, into this country.

Either these 2 Idiots were just stupid, or maybe they just didn't have mirrors at home. Maybe they just liked attention, we'll never know. My guess is that they were both paid well to run. That way the republicans looked like they believed in Diversity, while at the same time knowing they would only nominate a white candidate. Well, I think I'm going to wind down this little experiment in journalism, on President Obama's birthday. Yes, today he made 53 years old. I just hope like hell he makes 54. That may sound ominous, but there's a whole lot of hate out there being constantly instigated by the "Republican HATE MACHINE". I'm truly surprised that there has been no attempt on president Obama's life, yet. I truly believe that people like Russ Limburg, (I know that's not the way you spell his name. I just think he "STINKS"). constantly beat the drums on their right wing Hate shows, in the hope that one of their Brainwashed, ignorant, piece of shit followers, or Zombies will get the hint. I'll bet the secret Service have never worked this hard in the history of their agency's existence. I predict that one of their agents will write a book, in about a year or 2 after he leaves office detailing how hard it was trying to keep Obama alive during his 2 terms in office. Anyway, HAPPY BIRTHDAY MR PRESIDENT, AND MAY YOU HAVE MANY MORE. I know I disappointed a lot of you hard right republican Idiots, who were stupid enough to think, that you were about to read about a Black Man who Hated Obama as much as you do, but I was just pulling your leg. I know the things I said about impeaching Obama, and the subjects I used for his impeachment are things that you advocate, and you would NEVER IMPEACH HIM FOR THOSE THINGS. Actually, some of the things I said about impeaching Obama, have a little merit to them, especially the part about Bush, and Cheney. I know you right wing, Bush loving Clowns, who still think that bush was the greatest president in U.S history, hate it that you may have bought this book, but don't worry, at the rate things are going, the brain dead tea baggers are going to push the weak, spineless, do nothing republican congress to Impeach Obama anyway, they don't need my help. Every reason that I gave that the republicans could use against Obama was a laundry list of republican "Crimes" .For those of you who aren't very bright, let me explain. Obama failed, or refused to prosecute Bush, and Cheney. That in itself could possibly be "dereliction of duty", in other words, he violated the rules of the Geneva convention. The Geneva convention says that in the case of any Government torturing "prisoners of war", that that government has the duty of turning over the people responsible *for that torture. Section 2340 of the federal criminal code makes it an offense to "torture", or "conspire to torture". If a prisoner of war dies as a result of torture, the violators can be subject to lengthy jail terms, or the death penalty in some cases. It also says that the United States Government or any country for that matter has promised to prosecute, or extradite those who commit, or are "complicit in the commission of torture". It wouldn't be hard to argue that Bush, and Cheney are candidates for this law. First, they admit on public TV that they approved of, and knew of the waterboarding, and "enhanced interrogation of the prisoners being held in Guantanamo Bay, even until this very day, there are people being held in Guantanamo Bay, who have been there for years, and have never been tried. If these were American Citizens, there would be Hell to pay, and MILLIONS of dollars to pay in Lawsuits.*

JAMES WITHERSPOON

Yet, we wonder why other countries around the world HATE Americans. What they don't know is they don't have a reason to hate all Americans, "JUST OUR POLITICIANS" .Anyway, as I said, there are legitimate reasons to "IMPEACH OBAMA", but not the ones that the republicans preach about, they are Garbage, and made up. Impeach Obama for letting young, Black kids rot in jail for nothing. No, that wouldn't work because republicans approve of him doing that."IMPEACH OBAMA", for letting wall street get away with robbing the citizens of this country, and nobody going to jail, or facing anything other then fines. NO, that wouldn't work because republicans approve of that also. When it all boils down to Impeaching Obama for anything, it's not going to work. Mainly because the republicans have manipulated Obama into a position where they can't legitimately IMPEACH him for anything, without Dumping on their own policies, and their own people. In other words, he has supported everything they stand for, and now they want to impeach him for doing it. I could go on and on about the many reasons that Obama could be Impeached, but I don't think they would go for it. As I finish this book, the republicans are now suing Obama. I don't feel much sympathy for Obama for the simple reason that I believe that Obama, has brought a lot of this animosity on himself. Obama, for some reason, didn't seem to realize that you don't accommodate "BULLIES". The only way that you get along with Bullies is to "BEAT THE FUCK OUT OF THEM". The republicans knew that from the time he was elected, that he was going to try to be their friend, and they weren't going for it. All of the ass kissing that Obama has done, has produced ZERO. It has accomplished absolutely

NOTHING, as far as they are concerned, and I doubt if the next 2 years can erase that effect. Just because OBAMA is a black man doesn't mean that he thinks like a black man. I've come to the conclusion that the reason Obama has allowed the republicans to kick him in the ass, over and over again is because he has never lived the Black experience, and therefore didn't see it coming. He actually thought that if he was Civil, and didn't rile them up, that they would negotiate with him. What he didn't realize was that these people have a history of ingrained racism. Their Philosophy is never give in to reason, their philosophy is "we are superior", and no smart ass "NIGGER" is ever going to tell us any different. I don't blame Obama for not having a hard, black life. What I blame Obama is for, not doing a little research. Obama is "NOT" a typical Black Man. Obama really doesn't understand black people, and it shows, neither is BILL COSBY, but Cosby seems to identify more with black people, then Obama. Other then criticizing black fathers, Cosby is totally Gung ho for his people. This is evident, by the huge amounts of money, he has spent supporting the UNITED NEGRO COLLEGE, and other Black causes From what I understand, Cosby has spent over Half a billion dollars supporting black causes. I truly wish Cosby would sit down, and have a talk, with some of those other super rich black people, who don't seem to have any LOYALTY to their own people. You know the ones I'm talking about. Yes, I'm talking about the OPRAH WINFREYS of the black race. I know their aren't any other BLACK BILLIONAIRES out there, but there are a awful lot of black MILLIONAIRES out there who could get together, and maybe open up a large food store chain, something that could open up some jobs for black people. I understand that their money is their money, and they can do what they want with it, but there should be some inking of racial pride, in them somewhere. Instead, the few blacks who do have an ounce of entrepreneurism in their bones invest in things like clothing stores that blacks can't even afford to shop in unless they're RAPPERS. After all, blacks, me included, take pride in our athletes, and any other black person who makes it big. We make them our Heroes, because we know that they had to EXCEL, in whatever field they succeeded in, to be where they are. We don't need $100 gym shoes with our heroes name on them, we need JOBS. Poor blacks can't afford $100 gym shoes anyway, but the middleclass blacks waste their money on them as some kind of status symbol. We don't have a large black middleclass anyway. The myth that there is a large Black middleclass is not true. Most Black people are still struggling, and *will continue to struggle as long as we have politicians who act like the "Blacks are taking over the country". This is a republican talking point. From Reagan on down, they have used "Black prosperity" (what little we have), as a wake up point to white people. As long as they can act like black people have elevated to a point of middle class prosperity, they can say, "see, look at how black people have taken your white taxpaying dollars and enriched themselves"."They live like Kings, and Queens off food stamps", while you suffer". This isn't just racism. It's also class warfare. Now, you have the "poorest of the poor', against the 'poorest of the poor". You also have to be mighty dumb to believe that. WAIT A MINUTE,"NEWS FLASH". ANOTHER UNARMED, 18 YEAR OLD BLACK KID HAS BEEN MURDERED BY ANOTHER WHITE COP.THIS KID WAS EXECUTED IN BROAD DAYLIGHT,WITH*

WITNESSES EVERYWHERE AGAIN.THESE COPS ARE REALLY FEELING THAT IT'S OPEN SEASON ON YOUNG BLACK MEN .This time it happened somewhere called Ferguson, Missouri, right outside St Louis Mo. I'm not making this stuff up, it's really true. These racist ass cops are having a ball killing Black people. Maybe I shouldn't be passing judgment so early, but I have a feeling this is going to be another policeman cover up story. It seems the police left this kids body out in the open, in a puddle of blood, for over 5 hours while they are trying to figure out how to make this a legitimate MURDER. A few days have passed by, and now the police are saying this kid stole some cigars, or cigarillos, or something. Their original story was that he was walking in the middle of the street with a friend, and the cop told them to get out of the street. Either way, I didn't know it was a

JAMES WITHERSPOON

capital offense to shoplift, or walk in the middle of the street. At any rate, I didn't know that either one was punishable by DEATH. By the way, they're calling this shop lifting incident, a ROBBERY. How convenient. They have released some video of this kid pushing the store owner away as he exits the store. Somehow they've made that a ROBBERY, instead of shoplifting. The news media as usual, is helping the police spread their lies by steadily calling it a robbery, as if they work for the police department. The citizens of Ferguson are furious, and are rioting, for the 3rd day in a row. This could get very ugly. Meanwhile, Obama, and Eric Holder, and his injustice department are mute as usual. Obama hasn't contacted the dead kids parents, to give his condolences, or at least support, and Eric Holder is mum so far as to whether this boys civil rights were violated. Yes, I do know a lot about the law,

JAMES WITHERSPOON

because I had a lot of dealings with the courts in my life, as most black men have. Like the old saying goes, "I went to court today, and there was "Justice there". Richard Pryor said it right when he said it was "JUST US, there", meaning the court was full of just Black people. Anyway, today is about the 5th day of this MURDER, and the cop is still walking the streets, and the Police chief, and his cop buddies are trying to smear this kid as much as possible. I'm waiting for them to start talking about how many drugs were in his body as though that has any meaning whatsoever, about why this Cop MURDERED this kid. They know marijuana stays in your system for months, if not years, so I expect that to surface soon. They did that to justify killing Travon Martin also. In other words, these kids are responsible for their own deaths, because they smoked a joint. The details of this boys killing are "Horrendous".

JAMES WITHERSPOON

This cowardly, piece of shit cop, shot this kid 6 times, including twice in the head. He even shot him in the top of his head, as he was falling to the ground. I see why those people in Ferguson are rioting everyday. This shit is going from Bad to worse. The people in Ferguson have the right to be angry. That dead kid could have been any one of their kids."ANOTHER NEWS FLASH, ROBIN WILLIAMS, THE COMEDIAN HAS DIED.THEY THINK HE COMMITED SUICIDE BY HANGING HIMSELF, OR CUTTING HIS WRIST, OR SOMERTHING. Now here's where Obama is about to get caught up in another one of his ass kissing episodes again. You know he has to go on public TV and mourn for Robin Williams, and his family. He knows that if he doesn't show sorrow, and compassion for Robin Williams and his Family, the Faux follies anti news station, will say he hates white people again, and nothing is further from the truth. He loves white people a lot more then he loves Black people. Sure enough, Obama came on TV today, and expressed his concern for Robin Williams, and his family, and oh, by the way, he feels the pain of the MURDERED, dead kids parents also. That dead kids name is Michael Brown JR, Mr. OBAMA. Obama knew that he was caught in a bad situation. How was he going to show sympathy for this dead, rich, white man, who killed himself, but not show any compassion for the poor, 18 year old MURDERED BLACK KID? Obama knew that the black community all over the country could not help but notice that he had said absolutely NOTHING about the DEAD BLACK KID MURDERED BY THE COP. I wonder if Obama would have ever mentioned MICHAEL BROWN JR'S name if Robin Williams had not killed himself? He probably heard that a lot of Democrats, and the people on MSNBC, were beginning to wonder where he stood on this EXECUTION STYLE, MURDER BY a COP. While I'm talking about this, I have to say a few things about AL Sharpton that might not be nice. Al Sharpton   somehow went out and found the other kid who was with Michael Brown at the time of his execution, and put him on nationwide TV. He had this boy to sit up on television, in front of the whole world, and tell his whole eyewitness account of what happened that day. I'm sure MSNBC has attorneys at their beck and call. Why didn't anyone tell dumb ass Al Sharpton that you're not supposed to let eye witnesses get on TV and disclose everything they know, or saw? Right now, the attorneys for the Killer cop are watching that tape, and figuring out how to nullify everything that boy has said on TV. I know this had to seem strange to someone besides me. I also wish the talking heads on MSNBC would stop advancing that lie about this boy "ROBBING" a store for a pack of cigarillos. If anything, he shoplifted a pack of cigarillos. It was not a ROBBERY, as they all keep saying. This is what the Police WANT them to say. in the meantime, the KILLER COP is still running around loose somewhere on paid vacation, while the rioters, riot every night. They have no intention of arresting this crazy ass motherfucking cop. As usual the KILLER COP UNION is backing him to the fullest extent of their power. They as always, are on the side of cops that kill innocent black people. Today, I heard, or read on the internet that Obama as usual, meekly mentioned that Eric Holder was going to actually go to the scene of the crime, and do some investigating for a change, after all of these days of rioting. I guess they couldn't ignore this situation any longer. At the same time, he naturally had to "strongly" CONDEMN the rioters. His usual false Equivalency narrative that he uses on black people all of the time. It's always the black mans fault as much as it is the white mans fault who are victimizing black people. In other words, the victims are as much to blame, as the perpetrators. That way, he doesn't look like he's defending black people. The rioting seems to be calming down a bit, just because they got a little attention from the white house, and the DOJ. However, I wouldn't build up a whole lot of hope about that, if I were a Ferguson citizen. "NEWS FLASH". "An American journalist has been "BEHEADED" by ISIS", the terrorist group over there in Iraq. It seems they EXECUTED an American citizen because they didn't like Obama calling air strikes against them. They then uploaded the execution to the internet so that the world could see their handiwork

.These Animals deserve every bomb that we drop on them. Obama has already hit the airwaves with his outrage, and indignation, against the low life's that did this. I've never seen Obama this mad before. All of the news people are saying the same thing. Obama didn't wait a week to notify his family, and give his condolences like he did with the Brown Family. He was Johnny on the spot. He knew what he had to do, and he did it. Obama is going to go crazy trying to bring these terrorists to justice. He'll restart the Iraq war all over again to prove he means business. I agree with this wholeheartedly. My only question is; Why isn't Obama that hell bent for leather over bringing the Michael Brown MURDERER TO JUSTICE? I hope you see where I'm going with this; Obama waited a WEEK, before he even mentioned the Brown Murder. I don't believe he would have ever said anything if there wasn't so much rioting going on, and it wasn't in the news day in, and day out. Yet, he's willing to quietly, and meekly say "let the courts take care of this" about the Brown MURDER. He has shown no outrage over this boys Death. I know he can't come out and tell the truth. That COPS ARE THE BIGGEST LOWLIFES IN AMERICAN SOCIETY. However, he can show outrage when they OUTRIGHT MURDER AMERICAN CITIZENS. I don't think most people would hold that against him. I'll tell you why he's so weak, and timid about this outrage. It's because he knows that a large part of the American public condones what COPS DO TO BLACK PEOPLE. He also knows in his heart that he lacks the courage to try to do anything about it. He also knows that he is as much to blame for income inequality as George Bush was. Under Bush, the rich got richer, and the poor got poorer, with the help of the Bush tax cuts, that Obama kept renewing, the gap widened. With the good jobs that Bush lost Obama has replaced them with low paying service jobs. Just what the big corporations wanted. Big business has done great with Bush, and Obama. Wall Street should love Obama, they've done great. The big banks continue on as if nothing ever happened, not one person went to jail for their crimes and the billionaires made more billions, and the millionaires made more millions. Even the insurance companies took on millions of new customers with Obamacare. At least someone besides rich people benefit from Obamacare. If you left that up to republicans that wouldn't be possible either. The oil companies are still receiving corporate welfare in the billions, as the powers that be throw women and children off food stamps to pay for their oil subsidies .Yes, not a whole lot has changed. I believe that the only way we will ever see real change is if someone like Bernie Sanders, or Elizabeth Warren were to be elected as president. Obama has always been too close to Wall Street as well as Eric Holder. Hillary Clinton has already sold her soul to wall street, and big money, and I don't believe the republicans are going to work with her any better then they did with Obama. The Supreme Court has long sold out to the highest bidder, and this country doesn't look like it's going anywhere but down. As long as we're being distracted by endless war, and trying to police the world, we'll never advance like the rest of the world. We actually have a political party that seeks to destroy this country, and this Government. A party that long ago sold its soul to the Plutocrats and big money in general. Have you noticed that only the people from super poor countries are the only ones beating down our borders to try to get in here. People from prosperous countries don't even look our way.

JAMES WITHERSPOON

Those are the people from socialistic countries where everybody has a chance, and everybody is treated fairly. Most of them never tolerated slavery, or practiced Genocide like this country did against the American Indians. Yet, we've been brainwashed into believing that we're number 1 in the world in everything. We're not #1 in the best education. We're not #1 in healthcare. We're not #1 in good wages. We're not #1 in safety nets for our citizens. We're e not #1 in anything that's good for our citizens. We're #1 in the world for imprisoning our citizens. We're #1 for Murders of our citizens. We're #1 for our people dying for lack of healthcare. And we're #1 for income inequality. When you look at all of the racist bullshit that's going on today, you realize that nothing much has changed. Instead of stringing blacks up to the nearest tree, now they have the Gestapo type police to gun Blacks down in cold blood,

JAMES WITHERSPOON

while preaching human rights to the rest of the world. However, one thing about that situation going on in ST Louis with the rioting and all, kind of gets my goat. The town of Ferguson is 2/3 black, or about 70% black. How in the fuck can these people be so fucking stupid, that they have a WHITE MAYOR, A WHITE POLICE CAPTAIN, A WHITE CITY COUNCIL, and whites in all of the important places. How is this fucking possible? I'll tell you how. They're too fucking stupid to stop whatever the fuck it is that they're doing, and VOTE. They could vote everybody and anybody out of office that they want out of office. Things like this, are the reasons that White people think that Blacks are so STUPID. You can't really blame them. I heard that the republicans were furious because some smart Democrats set up some voter registration booths on the main drag during the rioting. The republicans are thinking the same thing that I'm thinking. THEY DON"T HAVE TO TAKE THIS SHIT. They are the majority in that town. What the fuck is wrong with these people? After all of the rioting cools down, and they find this MURDEROUS DOG innocent of killing this kid, maybe, just maybe, they'll come to their senses and VOTE. Ferguson is just a microcosm of Chicago, my home town. You have all of the same institutionalized racism, except on a grander scale. There's no excuse for Chicago having a white Mayor. Chicago's mayor was elected because the blacks in Chicago voted against their own best interests. They voted for Rahm Manuel because they thought he was a good friend of Obama's, now they're stuck with him. I hope in the next election, they have enough common sense to run just 1 black man, or woman against him, not 2 or 3. This isn't rocket science, just use your fucking head. We will

NEVER get any respect until we start thinking, and thinking as a people, not just as individuals. The Mexicans do it. The whites do it. The Asians do it. Everybody does it EXCEPT BLACKS. Until we reach that plateau, where we can think on that level, we will continue to commit black on black crime, Kill each other on an everyday basis, rot in jail for nothing, live in ghettos in sub standard housing, and be the victims of not just the white mans racism, but our own short comings. The things happening in Ferguson Missouri might be the beginning of a long overdue awakening for Blacks in America. Maybe this was the last straw, maybe not. I think that maybe I've gotten a little bit off target. This book is supposed to be all about Politics, but if you look at the overall picture, you can see how ignoring politics, can have a devastating effect on your life. Some people can't connect the dots between politics, and their everyday lives, especially black people. They don't realize the strength they have in sticking together, and voting in EVERY ELECTION. That means voting for aldermen, city council people, and sheriffs, anything you can vote on. Those people in Ferguson Mo are actually responsible for everything the racist ass cops, state prosecutors, mayor, Governor, and anybody who has anything to do with this mess, has done to them. I noticed on the news reports the other day, that they brought in a Black State trooper or something, who calmed these people down, and actually stopped them from rioting. He was hugging, and kissing people like they were members of his family. You could tell they loved this man, and trusted him. The first thing that I thought about was; Why isn't this man MAYOR, or POLICE CHIEF, or somebody in a powerful position in that town, who could have stopped this systemic RACISM, a long time ago? Well, I'm going to TRY to answer my own question. My guess is: Mr Johnson, (the trooper), was aware that the people in this town, had a dismal voting record in the past, something like a 6% turnout. Knowing that, he probably didn't have much confidence that he could win a political campaign within the black neighborhoods. It speaks volumes when you have a majority like that yet, every important political office   is held by the minority. It simply means that the minority is voting, and the Majority is NOT VOTING. How can you expect to get any RESPECT, when people know you're that stupid? My advice to the Black citizens of Ferguson is, put down the bricks, the Molotov cocktails, and the rocks. They will only get you KILLED. Did Mike Brown even have a brick in his hand when he was murdered? Of course not. Those COWARDS, masquerading as police officers, will KILL YOU FOR NOTHING. Pick up a book, and learn how to navigate the political process. Don't give them an excuse to MURDER YOU. Underneath all of that body armor, helmets, bullet proof vests, lies the hearts of COWARDS. Even with all that fire power made for Armies, not police officers, these so called police officers, say they're afraid of unarmed black kids. That should tell you a lot about those "brave "policemen in Ferguson. What would have happened if some of those "Black" protesters had brandished open carry weapons like the white people did in the Clive Bundy case in Nevada? I think we all know the answer to that one. There would have been a MASSACRE. There would have been DEAD PEOPLE EVERWHERE. Obama would have been on TV the next day saying it was the Black peoples fault because they shouldn't have been carrying guns. The republicans would have given him a few brownie points for killing some NIGGERS, and everybody would have been happy. White people came armed to the teeth, aiming sniper rifles at federal agents, over some fucking COWS, to protect a mans right not to pay his bills, and nothing happens. Black people come to a protest over the MURDER of an unarmed black kid and they get GASSED, BEATEN, and locked up. Maybe the armed militias have a point there. You don't take BRICKS, and BOTTLES to a GUNFIGHT, YOU TAKE GUNS. To this day, not 1 person has been arrested, or charged by Eric Holders non justice dept. You also haven't heard a big outcry from the republicans over this armed insurgency by these white people either. The news stations are quiet, and the newspapers are even quieter. Why isn't anybody demanding JUSTICE? You have big shot newspapers like the New York TIMES, vilifying and talking about unarmed, DEAD Mike Brown, not being such a ANGEL, yet, they're MUTE when it comes to white people threatening police with GUNS. These are the same people that will tell you that there is no thing as WHITE PRIVILEGE. These are the same people that will tell Black people to "stop Whining", and that includes OBAMA. This might sound like a joke, but "I have a dream", I can see Clarence "Uncle" Thomas retiring from the supreme court in about 10 years. Naturally, they want another token Black man on the Supreme Court, so they nominate Obama. The Republicans liked the way they had control over Obama when he was president so they confirm Obama in record time. They know Obama is on the side of big pharmacy, the insurance companies, the oil companies, and Wall Street just like they are. All of a sudden, out of the blue, my dream changes. I see Elizabeth Warren being inaugurated as president, Bernie Sanders, is vice President, and Anthony Weiner is Speaker of the house. In my dream, I see the Democrats controlling everything just like they did when Obama was elected President. However, I dream that Elizabeth Warren don't give a flying fuck about what the republicans think or say. She rams through all kinds of bills for jobs, single payer healthcare for the whole country, raises the minimum wage, stops giving Billions in oil subsidies, to the oil companies, puts Alan Grayson in charge of the DOJ ,and starts perp walking all of the criminals on Wall street out in Handcuffs. I Dream that the Democrats grow some balls, and make it against the law for any state to try to restrict people from voting. It would be a felony for anyone to file phony lawsuits that cost the taxpayers millions of dollars for nothing. You would be charged with treason if you tried to shut down, or

JAMES WITHERSPOON

even talked ill of the federal Government, while collecting taxpayer's money on your paycheck. You would be tried for treason and hung by the balls, (or Clitoris), in some cases, if you tried to stop people from receiving their social security checks, or Medicare. In my dream, those cowardly ass police officers who gun poor people down like animals, would be given twice as much time as the average lay person, because they were sworn to uphold the law, and instead, used their position of authority, and trust to kill innocent people. Plus they would have to serve their time in the very same jails, and prisons, that they sent innocent people too. These corrupt ass motherfuckers would get a chance to go one on one with the people they made criminals out of. Then we could see how tough these pieces of shit are without a Gun, and badge to protect them. Time to wake up, that won't happen in my lifetime, or even in this century.

JAMES WITHERSPOON

Then again, man seems to be advancing by leaps and bounds,(in some countries anyway},certainly not here, in the United States. In this country we seem to be standing still, as if we're in a time warp that won't be allowed by the republicans to move, until Obama is totally out of office. This country's Republican Party seems to be out to prove to the world that nothing has changed in this country's RACIST HISTORY. They have proven that they would rather see every man, woman, and child in this country suffer because a BLACK MAN is P.O.T.U.S.As I bring this book to an end, there are a few more things I want to bring out into the open that might be a little uncomfortable for some of you die hard Obama fans. Since Obama has been in office, everything good that could happen to the ultra rich people has happened. The billionaires have MORE BILLIONS, the millionaires have MORE MILLIONS, Wall street has money to burn to buy our politicians with, the oil companies, and insurance companies are making more money then ever before in history. To make a long story short, THE HAVES HAVE MORE, AND THE HAVE NOTS, HAVE LESS, good job Obama. Since Obama has been in office, Blacks, and other minorities have sunk deeper into poverty, what little they had has been taken away from them. Poor people in general, not just Blacks, are suffering more now then ever before. There are a lot of poor whites who are suffering just as much as black people. POVERTY HAS NO COLOR. Now, don't think that I'm saying this is all Obama's fault, because that's not true. What's Obama's fault is not taking advantage of the short time in office where he COULD HAVE CHANGED SOME THINGS. During that short period of time he squandered his advantage, trying to prove to the republicans, (and white people in general), that he was NOT a BLACK PRESIDENT, THAT WOULD TRY TO HELP HIS PEOPLE OUT OF POVERTY. I personally think he proved his point. He is going to leave office HATED BY THE SAME PEOPLE THAT HATED HIM WHEN HE WENT INTO OFFICE. He didn't make any friends with those people that he tried to befriend at the expense of the people who elected him. That was a lesson in futility, or it should have been anyway. After all he did for Bush, and Cheney, what did he get in return? Both of these CRIMINALS should be in jail today. Absolutely NOTHING, but criticism, for being too weak to prosecute them, especially from Cheney. After all of the sucking up to republicans, what did he get in return? HATRED. After criticizing, and lecturing Black Men about how to be better fathers, he still didn't get anything more then an "attaboy", from Republicans. The republicans did appreciate him stereotyping all black men, but they just couldn't bring themselves to pat him on the back in public, (they might have to physically touch him to do that), You can believe they enjoyed seeing Obama denigrating black fathers. They couldn't have said it better themselves. However, it's the same thing with IMPEACHMENT. The real reasons they should Impeach Obama has to do with the things I named like Bush, and Cheney, Wall street, hurting black kids, etc. They don't agree with those reasons because they are the architects of most of those things. Did you really think it was an accident that Obama kept Bushes war mongering Generals? Did you think it was an accident that Obama keeps republicans that served under Bush, in their positions today? Do you think that Obama had any qualms about extending the Bush Tax cuts for the rich? Do you think it's a coincidence that Obama supports the PATRIOT ACT, which allows the Government that the republicans "HATE SO MUCH", to spy on Americans? No, these things didn't happen by accident, they were PLANNED. Obama likes to BRAG that Obamacare was a republican Idea. He even tried to hang that albatross around Romney's neck, but Romney wasn't going to agree with Obama about anything, even if it made him look good. Obama even tried to show his undying LOVE for Ronald Reagan, (a man I despise), but the rethugs were not having that either. They probably were wondering why he had to suck up to a republican president, when he had so many GREAT Democratic Presidents to admire. I've often wondered about that myself. When I wonder about something, I usually try to figure it out. I've come up with this conclusion. OBAMA HAS NEVER REALLY BEEN A DEMOCRAT.

JAMES WITHERSPOON

AT MOST, HE IS A MODERATE REPUBLICAN. Obama knew before he ran for president that the ODDS of him running as a republican were nil to zero .Now, before all of you Blacks, progressives, liberals, and so on, have a heart attack, let me explain what I mean by that statement. I know what you're going to say. You're going to point out that Obama was a Democrat way back when he first started out as a community Organizer. This is true. However, Obama knew that he would have never got his political career off the ground if he had tried to run for any political office in the black neighborhoods of Chicago, as a republican, and that's a fact. He also knew that he would have to continue being a Democrat after he was elected to the senate. By then, Obama had a foothold in Politics, and there was no way he could maneuver his way into running as anything else. In Chicago the Black voting block is powerful, and Obama needed them. Obama also knew he probably would have gone a long way in the republican party, but he also knows that the republicans would have used him like they use ALL of their SO CALLED BLACK REPUBLICANS, AS TOKEN PAWNS. I thought it was Hilarious when I saw, and still see, minorities like Herman Cain, and Marco Rubio, run for president as republicans. It just tickles me to death. It's as though these guys don't have mirrors at home. Who knows, maybe it's profitable to be used as pawns. That being said, Obama also knew that the Democratic Party was his only hope of actually being taken seriously as a candidate for president. I really believe that Obama didn't really think he had a chance on the first try. I think he figured Hillary had too much Name recognition for him to really win. I thought maybe he was thinking about running, after Hillary had served her 8 years in office. After all, with the political climate the way it was at that time, and as young as he was, that wasn't a long time to wait to be President. It was a given that the American people were NOT going to put another republican back into office, no matter who he was. Then, of all people, war mongering John McCain pops up as the republican Candidate. He stupidly went out and found a dimwitted, Dingbat named Sarah Palin to offset Hillary's Gender. He actually thought that Hillary, not Obama, was going to be who he was going to be running against. I can imagine his great Joy, and surprise when it turned out to be Obama. I can see them high fiving in the republican camp over the thought that a BLACK MAN was the Democratic candidate for President. That was McCain's dream come true. He was going to win by a landslide. He just knew the country was NOT READY FOR A BLACK PRESIDENT. He knew that RACISM saturates this country like a possum saturates in its own RODENT GREASE. This was going to be a pushover. McCain had won the race before it started. Therefore, he felt safe beating the drums of indefinite war in Iraq, Afghanistan, and any other place he could start a war. He even went so far as to sing happily about "BOMB, BOMB, BOMBING, IRAN". He thought that was a real CATCHY tune. However, the American people didn't think it was so funny. McCain really thought he had the American voters by the Balls, so to speak. He figured that the American people had only one choice, and that was EITHER VOTE FOR ME, AND THE MILITARY COMPLEX, OR VOTE FOR THAT "NIGGER" .He knew the answer before he asked the question. There was no way that the racism that permeates this country was going to allow a black man to win against a white man. Then, to make matters worse, he allowed the "idiot" to open her vile, poisonous, racist, ass mouth. I don't think McCain had any idea how "STUPID" this woman really was. From the time she was allowed to talk, it was all downhill. I will always believe that McCain's running mate was a big part of the reason that he lost. However, all of the blame can't be attributed to Sarah Palin. Mainly, because McCain insisted on keeping the country in perpetual wars forever and the American people were tired of war. Also, McCain was a SICK, TIRED, OLD, MAN. Everybody with half a brain, had to be thinking, "what if McCain died in office?"The IDIOT", would be president of the United States. That had to be a problem for even the most dedicated racist to ponder. Nobody in their right mind wanted this scenario. RACE HATRED is one thing, annihilation of this whole country, and possibly the world, is yet another. You can bet

JAMES WITHERSPOON

that the whole world was watching this election, and crossing their fingers, that Obama would win. Anyway, Obama won, and now, it was time for the hard part. As much as you hear people talk about Obama is a liberal, I notice that I've never heard him say he was a liberal, or even a progressive. It's always someone else who's saying what he is. If it's a Democrat, they're HOPING he's a LIBERAL, OR PROGRESSIVE. If it's a republican, they're saying it like it's some kind of disease that Obama has. Obama has consistently tried to prove to the republicans that he isn't a liberal or a progressive. Now, here's where it gets tricky. Somehow, Obama manages to keep the liberals, and progressives at bay, and on his side, while at the same time trying to do everything he can to prove to the republicans, that he's really their friend also. The reason that I say he's a moderate republican is because Obama doesn't seem to mind sucking up to the republicans, at the expense of his base. He doesn't seem to care what his base thinks. He has to know it irritates his base for them to see him always kissing the republicans asses. Yet, after all is said and done, HIS BASE STILL LOVES HIM, INCLUDING ME. I still think his good deeds have outdone his mistakes. He has really done a lot for this country in spite of all of the obstruction he has faced from the Republican Party. While the fact remains that he could have done a lot more if he had come into the white house kicking ass, and taking names. I guess Obama did what he could without a real congress, and a not so strong, Democratic party. Let's face it; the Democrats have a big problem when it comes to messaging. They have absolutely no idea about how to market their strengths. They, and OBAMA, don't know how to tout their successes, or brag about their *accomplishments. They seem afraid to take credit for anything they do. As successful as Obama care is, you never hear of a Democrat embracing, and running for office on it. I guess they realize that just the mention of Obama's name is a turnoff to white audiences. Even in Kentucky, where you have some of the dumbest people in the country, the Democrat, MRS Grimes, is running against 'turtle", or Mitch McConnell, but is afraid to mention that Obamacare is a great success in that state. These Idiots of the country love "KNECT", even though they know in their hearts that it's Obamacare. That just really shows you the ignorance of some people. If Mrs. Grimes had a little courage, she could call Mitch out, by simply saying, "Are you going to kick hundreds of thousands of people off their healthcare because you hate Obama?" It would be a sure winner, but again, she's another Democrat without a backbone.*

Jelly Backbones; seem to run in the Democrats Genes. Well, I guess it's time to bring this to an end, so Ill end this by saying, I hope I tricked a lot of you Obama Haters into buying this book. If you liked it, burn it. Tell your friends about it but don't let them read your copy, make them buy their own, don't pass it around. I don't make any money that way. If you don't like it, use it for toilet paper, or to start your fireplace. You're probably a hateful, mean ignorant, son of a bitch anyway, and don't have any friends. If that's the case, trick one of your enemies into buying the book. Either way, I win. As for the people who still love Obama, Black or white, or any other color, or ethnicity, more power to you. You're not alone. I know I've been kind of hard on the brother, but I can't help but be truthful. I know a lot of you don't agree with me for whatever reason, but I don't want you to think that I have any malice toward

Obama. I'm still a loyal Obama voter, and I intend to always be by his side. However, you can be LOYAL, without being BLIND, and that's where I'm at. I also know I offended a lot of people with my over excessive swearing, and cursing, but that just the way I talk. I can hardly say a sentence without swearing one way or the other. However, if I offended a bunch of you holy rollers, it's too fucking bad. You need to take that fucking bible out of your hand, and replace it with some kind of book that's going to give you some real fucking knowledge. Also, you don't have to go vote, with a whole church load of fucking people. You can go by yourself. It irks the hell out of me, when I read that black people can't vote, because these racist ass motherfucking politicians are taking away Sunday voting because they know that's when black people go vote. Fuck that. Go voting anytime you get a chance. Vote from the privacy of your own home by absentee vote. Quit making excuses. What the fuck is so great about voting on Sunday anyway? Does it really make a difference? I can't possibly see why it would. Another thing, all black people should remember. The first thing, the slave owner did when he bought new slaves was to give them a BIBLE. THEY BETTER NOT HAVE LEARNED HOW TO READ IT, OR THEY WOULD HAVE BEEN HUNG. Yet, right today, you see black people all over the United States clinging to BIBLES, and BEGGING for some Invisible White man to save their soul. Now ,I'm not trying to make fun of church going people, I don't really give a flying fuck what anybody else believes in, that's their problem. However, I do take offense at all of those people who find it their business to try to convert me into their bullshit. Well that's enough talk about religion. To each his own. Well, I gave you my reasons why I think Obama should be impeached, and it's up to you to decide. I hope any republican who got a hold of this book by accident, or whatever, has a bad case of the shits, and shits in his pants for 2 weeks like that republican rock singer ,ted Nugent did to avoid the draft. As for you Obama, I wish you the best of luck, and I hope you make it out of office safely. You never know what these right wing terrorist nut jobs might do. I also hope the republicans give some thought to the ideas I presented on how to IMPEACH OBAMA. After all, nothing much that the republicans have said, or done has hurt the president much, maybe this will help them out. Of course I'm just joking. I wouldn't do anything to help anybody tarnish Obama's image. We already have a large percentage of the country that Hates Obama, for no other reason other then the fact, that he is Black. Most of these people are uneducated, ignorant, bigoted, church going, misinformed, watchers of FAUX Follies. They're failures by white people's standards, and they just have to have somebody to look down on. They don't have any better sense then to vote against their own best interests, and to me they're just downright STUPID. As I get ready to close this book out, I just can't help but say something about another young black man MURDERED by white Policemen. If this wasn't so tragic, it would be outright funny. The police in Louisiana arrested a young 22 year old black man for weed or something, and I think they allegedly found a little bit of cocaine. (I don't believe that for a minute). Anyway, after searching him, and handcuffing him in the back seat, somehow he shot himself in the back, or so they say. They actually want people to believe that this man committed suicide. This is another POLICE MURDER, of a young Black Man that I believe is actually inspired by POLICE HATRED of president Obama. As everybody knows, most policemen are republicans, and they're not the brightest people in the world. All Klansman's dream is to be a policeman, because they know they then have a license to KILL BLACK PEOPLE. I don't have respect for policemen, white, or black, because I've always had negative experiences with them. As a young Black man growing up in Chicago, I remember when Harold Washington, was elected as the first Black mayor of Chicago. The Chicago police WENT CRAZY. They would Harass black people for nothing, just out of spite, because HAROLD WASHINGTON WAS MAYOR OF CHICAGO. I remember being arrested 3 times in the first week of Harold Washington's election. Every time I was arrested, the arresting Officers would say shit like, "let's see your Black ass mayor get you out of this".

JAMES WITHERSPOON

"THIS", being "NOTHING, "because I hadn't done anything. I was released all 3 times, because I shouldn't have been arrested in the first place. This is the shit that most young black men, have to go through with the same POLICE that White people worship so much. Police seem to think that Black people in positions of power are going to hinder them from persecuting other blacks, and getting away with it. Therefore, they have to prove to the people that they are persecuting, that nothing has changed. In other words, just because a black man is now my boss, don't think for a minute that anything is going to change, we're still going to fuck over you. However, nothing is further from the truth. Once blacks get into power, they seem to just replace white skin with black skin. Blacks in power are no more likely to feel any kinship with another Black person then that white cop does, and in some cases they are worse. I believe this sudden rash of *BLACK MURDERS, AND EXECUTIONS BY COPS, Have a lot to do with OBAMA BEING PRESIDENT. They're trying to send a message to Black people that "NOTHING HAS CHANGED". Just because we have a black president, and the head of the DOJ is a black man, don't think for a second, that you're safe from us. GEORGE ZIMMERMAN WAS AN INSPIRATION TO THEM. They figure that, if any white citizen, can get away with MURDERING BLACK KIDS, I know I can, because I'm a cop, plus, I can get a PAID VACATION OUT OF THE DEAL. They're even KILLING BLACK MEN IN WAL-MART FOR LOOKING AT TOY GUNS. It's OK for white people to openly carry REAL GUNS, but a black man can't even look at a toy Gun, in the toy section of Wal-Mart? What the fuck is going on here? Well, I guess I've had* my rant. I could go on for days, and days, about the injustice in this supposedly free country, but I think I'll just write another book in my spare time. I want to see just how many of these COP MURDERERS, are going to be brought to justice by this administration. I know There's a time to speak, and a time not too, for a president, but how long can you sit back and watch your people be SLAUGHTERED by RACIST COPS? How long can you ignore the crimes of politicians in the name of bi-partisanship? How long can you allow Wall Street to steal without anyone being accountable, or going to Jail? How long can you hold young Black kids, in prison for what should be misdemeanor charges, and for something that is now legal in some states? Smoking a joint didn't ruin your life, so why should it ruin all of those young Black kids' lives? How long are you going to hold prisoners of war, in

Guantanamo Bay, who have been cleared of any wrongdoing, just to appease the republicans? It's time for this president to stand up to the republicans and defend the innocent people of this country who are being persecuted by a political Party that is RACIST, by anybody's standards. And yes, most of the injustice in this country is steeped in RACISM. It's time to quit ignoring it, and time to address it. If not now, WHEN? The Ball is in your court, and in your hands, are you going to SHOOT, or PASS IT? I think I know the answer, but I hope I'm wrong.